grzimek's
Student Animal Life Resource

• • • •

grzimek's
Student Animal Life Resource

• • • •

Amphibians
volume 1

New Zealand frogs to Australian toadlets

**Leslie A. Mertz, PhD, and
Catherine Judge Allen, MA, ELS, authors**

**Madeline S. Harris, project editor
Neil Schlager and Jayne Weisblatt, editors**

Detroit • New York • San Francisco • San Diego • New Haven, Conn. • Waterville, Maine • London • Munich

Grzimek's Student Animal Life Resource: Amphibians

Leslie A. Mertz, PhD, and Catherine Judge Allen, MA, ELS

Project Editor
Madeline S. Harris

Editorial
Stephanie Cook, Heather Price,
Lemma Shomali

Indexing Services
Synapse, the Knowledge Link
Corporation

Rights and Acquisitions
Margaret Abendroth, Timothy Sisler

Imaging and Multimedia
Randy Bassett, Michael Logusz, Dan
Newell, Chris O'Bryan, Robyn Young

Product Design
Tracey Rowens, Jennifer Wahi

Composition
Evi Seoud, Mary Beth Trimper

Manufacturing
Wendy Blurton, Dorothy Maki

LIBRARY OF CONGRESS CATALOGING-IN-PUBLICATION DATA

Mertz, Leslie A.
Grzimek's student animal life resource. Amphibians / Leslie A. Mertz and Catherine Judge Allen, authors; Neil Schlager and Jayne Weisblatt, editors.
     p. cm.
   Includes bibliographical references and index.
   ISBN 0-7876-9407-X (set hardcover : alk. paper) — ISBN 0-7876-9408-8 (volume
   1) — ISBN 0-7876-9409-6 (volume 2) — ISBN 0-7876-9410-X (volume 3)
   1. Amphibians—Juvenile literature. I. Allen, Catherine Judge. II. Schlager, Neil,
1966– III. Weisblatt, Jayne. IV. Title.
   QL644.2.M4263 2005
   597.8—dc22   2005015192

This title is also available as an e-book
Contact your Thomson Gale sales representative for ordering information.

Printed in Canada
10 9 8 7 6 5 4 3 2 1

Contents

AMPHIBIANS: VOLUME 3

Reader's Guide

Grzimek's Student Animal Life Resource: Amphibians offers readers comprehensive and easy-to-use information on Earth's amphibians. Order entries provide an overview of a group of families, and family entries provide an overview of a particular family. Entries are arranged by taxonomy, the science through which living things are classified into related groups. Each entry includes sections on physical characteristics; geographic range; habitat; diet; behavior and reproduction; animals and people; and conservation status. All entries are followed by one or more species accounts with the same information as well as a range map and photo or illustration for each species. Entries conclude with a list of books, periodicals, and Web sites that may be used for further research.

ADDITIONAL FEATURES

Each volume of *Grzimek's Student Animal Life Resource: Amphibians* includes a pronunciation guide for scientific names, a glossary, an overview of amphibians, a list of species in the set by biome, a list of species by geographic location, and an index. The set has 221 full-color maps, photos, and illustrations to enliven the text, and sidebars provide additional facts and related information.

NOTE

Grzimek's Student Animal Life Resource: Amphibians has standardized information in the Conservation Status section. The IUCN Red List provides the world's most comprehensive inventory of the global conservation status of plants and animals. Using a set of criteria to evaluate extinction risk, the IUCN recognizes the following categories: Extinct, Extinct in the Wild, Critically Endangered, Endangered, Vulnerable, Conservation Dependent, Near Threatened, Least Concern, and Data Deficient. These terms are defined where they are used in the text, but for a complete explanation of each category, visit the IUCN web page at http://www.iucn.org/themes/ssc/redlists/RL cats2001booklet.html.

ACKNOWLEDGEMENTS

Gale would like to thank several individuals for their assistance with this set. Leslie Mertz and Catherine Judge Allen wrote the text for the volumes. At Schlager Group Inc., Jayne Weisblatt and Neil Schlager coordinated the writing and editing of the set.

Special thanks are also due for the invaluable comments and suggestions provided by the *Grzimek's Student Animal Life Resource: Amphibians* advisors:

- Mary Alice Anderson, Media Specialist, Winona Middle School, Winona, Minnesota
- Thane Johnson, Librarian, Oklahoma City Zoo, Oklahoma City, Oklahoma
- Debra Kachel, Media Specialist, Ephrata Senior High School, Ephrata, Pennsylvania
- Nina Levine, Media Specialist, Blue Mountain Middle School, Courtlandt Manor, New York
- Ruth Mormon, Media Specialist, The Meadows School, Las Vegas, Nevada

COMMENTS AND SUGGESTIONS

We welcome your comments on *Grzimek's Student Animal Life Resource: Amphibians* and suggestions for future editions of this work. Please write: Editors, *Grzimek's Student Animal Life Resource: Amphibians*, U•X•L, 27500 Drake Rd., Farmington Hills, Michigan 48331-3535; call toll free: 1-800-877-4253; fax: 248-699-8097; or send e-mail via www.gale.com.

Pronunciation Guide for Scientific Names

Acanthixalus spinosus ay-kan-THICK-sal-us spy-NO-sus

Adelotus brevis ay-deh-LO-tus BREH-vis

Adenomus kandianus ay-deh-NO-mus kan-die-AY-nus

Albericus siegfriedi al-BEAR-ih-kus SIG-freed-eye

Alexteroon jynx ay-LEKS-tih-roh-on jinks

Allophryne ruthveni ah-lo-FRYN rooth-VEN-eye

Allophrynidae ah-lo-FRY-nih-dee

Alytes obstetricans ah-LYE-tes ob-STET-trih-kanz

Ambystoma tigrinum am-bih-STOH-ma tih-GRIH-num

Ambystomatidae am-bih-stoh-MA-tih-dee

Amphiuma tridactylum am-fee-U-ma try-DAK-tih-lum

Amphiumidae am-fee-U-mih-dee

Aneides lugubris ay-NEE-ih-deez lu-GU-bris

Ansonia longidigita an-SOH-nee-aye lon-jih-DIJ-ih-ta

Anura ann-UR-uh

Arenophryne rotunda ah-ree-no-FRYN roh-TUN-da

Arthroleptidae ar-throh-LEP-tih-dee

Arthroleptis stenodactylus ar-throh-LEP-tis sten-oh-DAK-tih-lus

Ascaphidae as-KAF-ih-dee

Ascaphus montanus as-KAF-us mon-TAN-us

Assa darlingtoni AY-suh dar-ling-TON-eye

Atelognathus patagonicus ay-teh-log-NAYTH-us pat-ah-GO-nih-kus

Atelopus varius ay-teh-LO-pus var-ee-us

Atelopus vogli ay-teh-LO-pus vohg-lye

Barbourula busuangensis bar-bo-RU-la bus-u-an-JEN-sis

Bolitoglossa pesrubra bo-LYE-toh-glos-sah pes-ROO-bra
Bombina bombina BOM-bin-ah BOM-bin-ah
Bombina orientalis BOM-bin-ah oh-ree-en-TAL-ihs
Bombina variegata BOM-bin-ah vay-ree-GA-ta
Bombinatoridae BOM-bin-ah-TOR-ih-dee
Brachycephalidae brak-ee-sef-FAL-ih-dee
Brachycephalus ephippium brak-ee-SEF-fal-us ee-FIP-ee-um
Brachycephalus nodoterga brak-ee SEF-fal-us no-DOE-tur-ga
Brachycephalus pernix brak-ee-SEF-fal-us PER-nicks
Brachycephalus vertebralis brak-ee-SEF-fal-us ver-teh-BRA-lis
Brachytarsophrys intermedia brak-ee-TAR-so-frys in-tur-ME-dee-uh
Bufo marinus BOO-foe MAYR-ih-nus
Bufo periglenes BOO-foe pair-ee-GLEH-nees
Bufonidae boo-FOH-nih-dee
Bymnophiona bim-no-fee-OH-nuh
Caecilian seh-SILL-ee-uhn
Caeciliidae seh-SILL-ee-eye-dee
Caudata kaw-DAY-tuh
Centrolene geckoideum SEN-troh-lean gek-oh-EYE-dee-um
Centrolenidae sen-troh-LEN-ih-dee
Ceratophrys cornuta seh-RAT-oh-fris kor-NEW-ta
Chioglossa lusitanica chee-oh-GLOSS-ah loo-sih-TAN-ih-ka
Cochranella ignota kok-ran-ELL-ah ihg-NO-ta
Cochranella saxiscandens kok-ran-ELL-ah saks-ee-SKAN-denz
Colostethus caeruleodactylus coh-loh-STETH-us see-RUE-lee-oh-DAK-til-us
Conraua goliath kon-RAH-u-ah go-LYE-eth
Cophixalus riparius co-FIX-ah-lus rih-PAIR-ee-us
Cryptobranchidae KRIP-toe-BRAN-kih-dee
Cryptobranchus alleganiensis krip-toe-BRAN-cus al-lee-GAY-nee-en-sis
Cyclorana platycephala sy-klo-RA-na plat-ee-SEF-fa-la
Cynops pyrrhogaster sy-NOPS pie-roh-GAS-ter
Dendrobatidae den-droh-BA-tih-dee
Dermophis mexicanus der-MO-fis meks-ih-KAN-us
Desmognathus fuscus dez-mog-NATH-us FUS-cus
Dicamptodon tenebrosus di-CAMP-toe-don ten-eh-BROH-sus
Dicamptodontidae di-CAMP-toe-DON-tih-dee
Discoglossidae dis-ko-GLOSS-ih-dee

Discoglossus pictus dis-ko-GLOSS-us PIK-tus

Edalorhina perezi ed-dah-LOR-heena PER-ez-eye

Epicrionops marmoratus eh-pee-KREE-oh-nops mar-moh-RA-tus

Epipedobates tricolor eh-pee-ped-oh-BA-tees tri-KUL-or

Eurycea bislineata u-REE-see-uh bis-LIN-ee-ah-ta

Eurycea rathbuni u-REE-see-uh rath-BUN-eye

Gastrophryne carolinensis GAS-troh-fryn kay-roh-LIN-en-sis

Gastrotheca riobambae gas-troh-THEH-ka ree-oh-BAM-bee

Gymnophiona jim-no-fee-OH-nuh

Heleophryne natalensis heh-lee-oh-FRYN nay-TAL-en-sis

Heleophrynidae heh-lee-oh-FRYN-ih-dee

Hemiphractus proboscideus heh-mee-FRAK-tus proh-BOSS-kid-day-us

Hemisotidae heh-mee-SAW-tih-dee

Hemisus barotseensis heh-MEE-sus bare-aht-SEEN-sis

Hemisus marmatorus heh-MEE-sus mar-mah-TOR-us

Hemisus sudanensis heh-MEE-sus soo-dan-EN-sis

Hyalinobatrachium valerioi high-ah-LIN-oh-bah-TRAK-ee-um vah-LAIR-ree-oh-eye

Hyla leucophyllata HIGH-lah loo-ko-fye-LAT-ta

Hylidae HIGH-lih-dee

Hynobiidae high-no-BEE-eye-dee

Hynobius retardatus high-NO-bee-us ree-tar-DAT-tus

Hyperoliidae high-per-OLE-lee-eye-dee

Hyperolius marginatus high-per-OLE-lee-us mar-jin-AT-tus

Hyperolius marmoratus high-per-OLE-lee-us mar-more-AT-tus

Hyperolius viridiflavus high-per-OLE-lee-us vir-rid-ih-FLA-vus

Ichthyophiidae ik-thee-oh-FYE-eye-dee

Ichthyophis glutinosus ik-thee-OH-fis gloo-tin-OH-sus

Kaloula pulchra kah-LOW-oo-la PULL-kra

Kassina senegalensis kah-see-na sen-ee-gall-EN-sis

Leiopelma hamiltoni lay-oh-PEL-ma ham-il-TO-nye

Leiopelma pakeka lay-oh-PEL-ma pa-KEY-ka

Leiopelmatidae lay-oh-pel-MAH-tih-dee

Lepidobatrachus laevis lep-ee-doh-bah-TRAK-us lay-EH-vis

Leptobrachium banae lep-toh-BRAK-ee-um BAN-nee

Leptodactylidae lep-toh-dak-TIL-ih-dee

Leptodactylus pentadactylus lep-toh-dak-TIL-us pen-ta-DAK-til-us

Limnodynastidae lim-no-dye-NAS-tih-dee

Lithodytes lineatus lih-thoh-DYE-teez lin-ee-AT-tus

Litoria caerulea lih-TOR-ree-uh seh-RU-lee-uh

Mantidactylus liber man-ti-DAK-til-us LEE-ber

Megophryidae me-go-FRY-ih-dee

Megophrys montana me-go-FRIS mon-TAN-ah

Micrixalus phyllophilus my-krik-SAL-us fye-LO-fil-us

Microbatrachella capensis my-kro-bah-trak-ELL-la cap-PEN-sis

Microhyla karunaratnei my-kro-HIGH-la kare-roo-nah-RAT-nee-eye

Microhylidae my-kro-HIGH-lih-dee

Myobatrachidae my-oh-bat-TRAK-ih-dee

Nasikabatrachidae nas-SIK-ka-bat-TRAK-ih-dee

Nasikabatrachus sahyadrensis nas-SIK-ka-bat-TRAK-us sa-HIGH-ah-dren-sis

Necturus maculosus nek-TOO-rus mak-u-LOH-sus

Neobatrachus pictus nee-oh-bat-TRAK-us PIK-tus

Notaden melanoscaphus NO-tah-den mel-an-oh-SKAF-us

Nyctixalus pictus nik-TIK-sal-us PIK-tus

Occidozyga lima ock-sih-DOZE-ih-gah LEE-ma

Onychodactylus japonicus on-ik-oh-DAK-til-us ja-PON-ih-kus

Oreolalax schmidti oh-ree-oh-LA-laks SCHMIDT-eye

Otophryne pyburni oh-toe-FRYN pie-BURN-eye

Parhoplophryne usambarica par-HOP low-fryn u-sam-BAR-ee-ka

Pelobatidae pel-low-BA-tih-dee

Pelodytes punctatus pel-low-DYE-teez punk-TAH-tus

Philautus papillosus fil-LAW-tus pa-pill-OH-sus

Philoria pughi fil-LOW-ree-uh PYU-eye

Phrynomantis bifasciatus fry-no-MAN-tis bi-FAS-see-at-tus

Phyllobates terribilis fye-low-BA-teez ter-rib-BIL-iss

Pipa pipa PIE-pa PIE-pa

Pipidae PIE-pih-dee

Plethodontidae pleth-oh-DON-tih-dee

Pleurodema bufonina PLOOR-oh-dee-ma boo-fo-NEE-na

Proteidae pro-TEE-ih-dee

Proteus anguinus PRO-tee-us AN-gwin-us

Pseudis paradoxa SOO-dis pair-ah-DOKS-sa

Pseudoeurycea bellii soo-doe-yur-EE-see-ah BELL-ee-eye

Rachophorus arboreus rak-OH-for-us ar-bor-EE-us

Rana catesbeiana RAH-nah kat-TEEZ-bee-eye-an-uh

Rana temporaria RAH-nah tem-po-RARE-ee-uh

Ranidae RAH-nee-dee

Ranodon sibiricus RAH-no-don sib-EAR-ee-kus

Rhacophoridae rak-oh-FOR-ih-dee

Rhinatrematidae rye-na-tree-MA-tih-dee

Rhinoderma darwinii rye-no-DER-ma dar-WIN-ee-eye

Rhinodermatidae rye-no-der-MA-tih-dee

Rhinophrynidae rye-no-FRY-nih-dee

Rhinophrynus dorsalis rye-no-FRY-nus DOR-suh-lis

Rhyacotriton cascadae rye-YA-koh-try-ton KAS-kah-dee

Rhyacotritonidae rye-ya-koh-try-TON-nih-dee

Salamandra salamandra sal-a-MAN-dra sal-a-MAN-dra

Salamandridae sal-a-MAN-drih-dee

Scaphiophryne calcarata skaf-FEE-oh-fryn kal-ka-RAT-ta

Scaphiophryne gottlebei skaf-FEE-oh-fryn got-LEB-ee-eye

Scaphiophrynidae skaf-fee-oh-FRYN-nih-dee

Scarthyla goinorum skar-THIGH-la go-in-OR-um

Scolecomorphidae skoh-lee-kom-MOR-fih-dee

Scolecomorphus kirkii skoh-lee-kom-MOR-fus KIRK-ee-eye

Silurana tropicalis sil-u-RA-na trop-ih-KAL-is

Siren intermedia SIGH-ren in-ter-ME-dee-uh

Sirenidae sigh-REN-nih-dee

Sooglossidae soo-GLOSS-sih-dee

Sooglossus sechellensis soo-GLOSS-sus say-shell-EN-sis

Stumpffia helenae STUM-fee-uh hell-LEN-ah-ee

Taudactylus eungellensis taw-DAK-til-us ee-u-jel-LEN-sis

Thoropa miliaris thor-OH-pa mil-ee-AIR-iss

Trichobatrachus robustus try-koh-ba-TRAK-us roh-BUS-tus

Triprion petasatus TRIP-pree-on pet-TAS-sah-tus

Triturus cristatus TRY-ter-us krih-STAT-us

Triturus vulgaris TRY-ter-us vul-GARE-iss

Tylototriton verrucosus tie-LOW-tow-try-tun ver-ruh-KOH-sus

Typhlonectes compressicauda tie-flo-NEK-teez kom-press-sih-KAW-duh

Uraeotyphlus oxyurus u-ray-ee-oh-TIE-flus oks-ee-YUR-us

Uraeotyphylidae u-ray-ee-oh-tie-FIE-lih-dee

Vibrissaphora ailaonica vie-brih-saf-FOR-uh ale-la-ON-nik-ah

Xenopus laevis zee-NA-pus lay-EH-vis

Words to Know

A

Adaptable organism An organism that can adjust to various living conditions.

Ambush A style of hunting in which a predator hides and waits for an unsuspecting prey animal to come to it.

Amphibian A vertebrate that has moist, smooth skin; is cold-blooded, meaning the body temperature is the same as the temperature of the surroundings; and, in most instances, has a two-stage life cycle.

Amplexus In frogs, a mating position in which the male clings to the female's back.

Amphipods Beach fleas, water lice, and other small water-living invertebrates.

Aposematic coloration Warning colors that advertise something about an animal, possibly its bad-tasting, poisonous skin.

Aquatic Living in the water.

Arboreal Living in trees.

Arthropods Insects, spiders, and other invertebrates that have jointed legs.

B

Balancers Structures on the sides of the head of some salamander larvae that support the head until the legs develop.

Barbels Little bits of flesh sometimes seen dangling from the mouth or chin of animals, such as some frogs and fishes.

Bask Sunbathe; often seen in reptiles and amphibians to help warm up their bodies.

Bioindicator species An organism that people can use to tell whether or not the environment is healthy.

Bromeliads Plants of warm, usually tropical, forests that often grow on other plants. Their leaves typically overlap into cup shapes that can hold water.

C

Cannibalistic Describing animals that eat other members of their own species.

Carnivorous Meat-eating.

Cartilage A flexible material in an animal's body that is often associated with bones.

Chorus In male frogs, a group that calls together.

Chromosomes The structures in a cell that hold the DNA.

Cloaca The chamber in some animals that holds waste from the kidneys and intestines, holds eggs or sperm about to be released to the outside, holds sperm entering a female's body, and is the passage through which young are born.

Coniferous forest Land covered with trees that bear their seeds inside cones.

Crepuscular Describing animals that are active only at dawn and at dusk.

Crustaceans Water-dwelling animals that have jointed legs and a hard shell but no backbone.

Cryptic coloration Colors and often patterns on an animal that help it blend into its environment.

Cutaneous respiration Breathing through the skin

D

Deciduous forest Land covered by trees that lose their leaves during cold or dry seasons.

Direct development Process by which frog eggs develop right into froglets and skip the tadpole stage.

Diurnal Active during the day.

DNA A chain of chemical molecules that is the instruction booklet for making a living thing; scientists can tell one species from another by comparing the DNA.

E

Ectothermic Describing animals whose body temperature changes when the outside air warms up or cools down.

Embryo A developing animal that has not yet hatched or been born.

Estivation As seen in some animals, a period of inactivity during dry spells.

Explosive breeders Members of a species that breed together in a large group, usually over a very short time.

F

Fertilization The joining of egg and sperm to start development.

Filter feeder An animal that strains water for bits of food.

Foraging Searching for food.

Fossorial Living underground.

Froglet The life stage of a frog right after the tadpole stage.

G

Gill An organ for obtaining oxygen from water.

Granular glands Poison glands, which in frogs are typically in noticeable bumps, often called "warts," on the back.

H

Herbivorous Plant-eating.

Herpetologist A person who studies amphibians and reptiles.

Hibernation A state of deep sleep that some animals enter in the winter to help them survive the cold weather.

Hybrid Describing the young produced by parents of two different species.

I

Indirect development Process by which frog eggs develop first into tadpoles and then into froglets.

Infertile eggs Eggs that will never develop into young.

Introduced species An animal, plant, or other species that is brought to a new location, usually by humans, either on purpose or by accident.

Invertebrate An animal, such as an insect, spider, or earthworm, without a backbone.

L

Larva (plural, larvae) An animal in an early stage that changes form before becoming an adult.

Lateral line system A row of tiny dot- or stitch-shaped organs, seen in fishes, tadpoles, and some other water-living organisms, that allow the animal to feel vibrations in the water.

M

Marsupium Found in some animals, a pouch in the adult where the young develop.

Metamorphosis The changes in form that some animals make to become adult, such as tadpole to frog.

Microorganisms Living things that are too small to see.

Mimic To copy.

Mollusk An animal with a soft, unsegmented body that may or may not have a shell.

N

Nocturnal Active mostly at night.

Nuptial pads Seen in some frogs, thick pads that form on the forelegs, on the front feet, on the toes of the front feet, and sometimes on the chest to help the male grip onto the female during mating.

O

Ocelli In frogs, small dots of color.

Opportunistic feeder An animal that will eat just about anything that it can capture and swallow.

Ovary The organ that makes eggs.

P

Palate The roof of the mouth.

Paratoid glands In some frogs, a pair of enlarged poison-containing sacs found at the back of the head.

Permanent body of water A body of water that is filled with water year-round.

S

Silt Dirt that is washed from land and collects in rivers and streams.

Sperm Microscopic cells from a male that trigger eggs from a female to start development.

Spicules Seen on the snout of a Mesoamerican burrowing toad, small, hard, sometimes pointy bumps.

Spine Backbone; also known as the vertebral column.

Spiracle In a tadpole, a tiny hole that lets water out.

Sternum A bone in the middle of the chest between the ribs; breastbone.

Symmetrical Describing a pattern that has two sides that are mirror images of one another.

T

Temporary body of water A body of water that is only filled with water for part of the year.

Terrestrial Living on land.

Toxin Poison.

Toxicity The level of poison.

Transparent See-through.

Tubercles Bumps.

Tympanum Eardrum, which in many frogs is visible as a round spot on the side of the head.

U

Utraviolet radiation A type of light that humans cannot see, but that scientists believe may be harming some frog species, especially those that live high in mountains where the radiation is strongest.

Unken reflex Seen in some frogs and salamanders, a stiff back-bend pose that serves to warn predators that the animal is bad-tasting or poisonous.

Urostyle A long, rod-shaped bone in the hip area of a frog.

V

Vernal pool A body of water that forms in the spring but then dries up for the rest of the year.

Vertebrae The bones that make up the spinal column.

Vertebrates Animals, such as birds, frogs, snakes, and mammals, with backbones.

Vocal sac Extra flesh on the throat of most male frogs that expands like a balloon when they make their calls.

Wart In frogs, a wart is a lump in the skin that contains poison and helps protect the frog from predators. In humans, a wart results from a virus and sometimes requires medical care.

Getting to Know Amphibians

Three different types of amphibians (am-FIB-ee-uhns) live on Earth today:

- Frogs are the often-slimy creatures almost everyone has seen hopping into a pond or heard calling on a spring evening. The smallest species reach less than one-half an inch (1.3 centimeters) long, while the largest can grow to more than a foot (30.5 centimeters) in length. Frogs are in the order Anura (ann-UR-uh). Toads are included in this order, too. They are simply one kind of frog. Frogs are different from other amphibians because they do not have tails when they are adults. Some frogs, called the tailed frogs, have little taillike bits of tissue, but they are not really tails. Many frogs have long and strong hind legs for hopping, but a few have short hind legs and typically get around by walking or running.

- Salamanders are the four-legged, tailed animals that hikers or gardeners sometimes surprise when they turn over a rock or log. The smallest salamanders are less than 1.2 inches (3 centimeters) long, while the largest can grow to 4 feet 11 inches (150 centimeters) in length, or more. Salamanders have bodies in the shape of a pipe with a tail at the rear. Most have small legs that are all about the same size. They hold their legs out to the side of the body when they are scrambling around on the ground. A few species have only two legs. The name of the salamanders' order is Caudata (kaw-DAY-tuh).

- Caecilians (seh-SILL-ee-uhns) come in many sizes, ranging from just 4.5 inches long to more than 5 feet 3 inches (160 centimeters) in length, but most people have never seen them in the wild. Caecilians look rather like earthworms, even having similar rings around their bodies, but caecilians have many things that earthworms do not, including jaws and teeth. A caecilian's tail is actually quite short, but since it blends into the rest of the body, this can be difficult to see unless the animal is flipped over. The tail in a caecilian begins at the vent, a slitlike opening on its underside. The caecilians are in the order Gymnophiona (jim-no-fee-OH-nuh).

In all, the world holds at least 4,837 species of frogs and toads, 502 of salamanders, and 165 of caecilians. Scientists are still discovering new species, so those numbers grow larger and larger as the years pass.

WHAT MAKES AN AMPHIBIAN AN AMPHIBIAN?

Although frogs, salamanders, and caecilians are usually not mistaken for one another, they still share several features that make them all amphibians.

Illustration of a frog skeleton. (Illustration by Marguette Dongvillo. Reproduced by permission.)

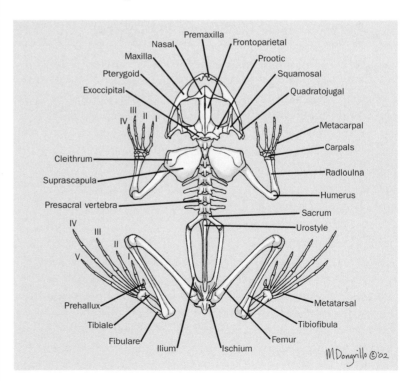

Skin

Some people confuse salamanders with lizards, but lizards are reptiles. An easy way to tell an amphibian from a reptile is to check for scales on the skin. Reptiles have scales, but amphibians do not. The skin of an amphibian is at least a little bit moist, even among the rather-dry toads, and some amphibians are very slippery. Part of the slipperiness comes from the moist or wet places they live, and part of it comes from their mucus (MYOO-kus) glands. Mucus glands are little sacks that ooze a slimy substance.

Amphibians also have another type of glands in their skin that ooze poison instead of mucus. Depending on the species, the poison may be weak or very strong. The poison in some of the poison frogs of South America is even powerful enough to kill a person who gets some in his or her bloodstream. In other species, just a little taste of the poison can turn a person's lips numb or cause extreme sickness.

Body temperature

Like fishes and reptiles, amphibians have body temperatures that become colder when the outside temperature is cold and warmer when the outside temperature is hot. Animals with a changing body temperature like this are known as ectothermic (EK-toe-thur-mik) animals. Sometimes, people call ectothermic animals "cold-blooded," but they are really only cold when the weather is also cold. Many amphibians warm themselves by sunbathing, or basking. Frogs frequently sit on shore in damp but sunny spots to bask. They may also simply swim into the warmer, upper layer of water in a pond to heat themselves up a bit. When they get too hot, they typically move to a cooler place, sometimes even going underground. This not only keeps them cooler but also helps them stay moist, which is important for their breathing.

Breathing

Amphibians breathe in several different ways. Like reptiles, birds, and mammals, most amphibians breathe in air through their nostrils to fill up their lungs. Caecilians have two lungs, but the left one is much smaller than the right one. This arrangement works well for the caecilians, which would not have room for two large lungs in their long and thin bodies. Some salamanders have very small lungs, and a few, such as the red-backed salamander that is common in North American forests, have no lungs at all.

Small or no lungs does not cause a problem for amphibians, however, because they do much of their breathing through their skin. When a person breathes in through the nose, the air travels into the lungs in the chest, where blood picks up the oxygen from the air and delivers it throughout the body. In amphibians, oxygen can pass right through their moist skin and into blood that is waiting in blood vessels just below the skin. The skin must be moist for this process to work: A dry amphibian is a dead amphibian. Using this through-the-skin breathing, which is called cutaneous respiration (kyoo-TAIN-ee-us res-per-AY-shun), amphibians can even breathe underwater. Oxygen that is dissolved in the water can also cross the skin and enter their blood.

Most amphibians go through a phase in their lives when they breathe underwater through gills, just as a fish does. Gill breathing is like cutaneous respiration, because dissolved oxygen in the water is picked up by blood in vessels that are in the gills. Gills are so full of blood vessels that they are typically bright red. Usually an amphibian breathes through gills only when it is young. Frogs, for instance, use gills when they are still tadpoles. A young salamander, which also has gills, is called a larva (LAR-vuh). The plural of larva is larvae (LAR-vee). Some amphibians, however, skip the gill-breathing phase and hatch right from the egg into a lung- and/or skin-breather. Others, however, keep their gills throughout their entire lives. Mudpuppies are examples of a salamander that has gills even as an adult. Since they live in the water, gills work well for them. In a few species, like the eastern newt, the animal goes through several phases: a gill-breathing larva, then a gill-less juvenile, and finally a gilled adult.

Hearing

Besides hearing sounds like humans do, frogs and salamanders can hear vibrations in the ground. When the ground vibrates, the movement travels up their front legs to the shoulder blade and then to a muscle that connects to the ear, so the amphibian can hear it. This type of hearing can be very sensitive. Not only can amphibians hear the footsteps of an approaching predator, like a raccoon, but they can also hear something as slight as an insect digging in the soil.

WHERE AMPHIBIANS LIVE

Amphibians live around the world. The only places where they do not live are in the extremely cold polar regions of the Earth, most of the islands in the ocean, and some desert areas. The three major groups of amphibians—the frogs, the caecilians, and the salamanders—each have their own favorite climates. Caecilians stay in warm, tropical climates and nowhere else. Although frogs live just about anywhere an amphibian can live, the greatest number of species make their homes in the tropics. Salamanders, on the other hand, tend toward cooler areas. Most salamanders live north of the Equator, and many exist in areas that have all four seasons, including a cold winter.

Because amphibians must keep their skin moist, they are always tied to water. That water may be a lake or river, a little puddle, a clammy spot under a log, or even a slightly damp burrow underground.

In the water

Most amphibians live at least part of their lives in the water. Many frogs and salamanders lay their eggs in the water. The frog eggs hatch into tadpoles, and the salamander eggs hatch into larvae. Both the tadpoles and the salamander larvae have gills that they use to breathe underwater. Eventually, the tadpoles turn into baby frogs, and the salamander larvae turn into young salamanders, and both can then leave the water to live on land. Scientists do not have all of the details about caecilians, but they think the typical caecilian lays its eggs on land; the eggs hatch into young that are also called larvae and have gills; and the larvae wriggle into water. The caecilian larvae grow in the water before losing their gills and moving onto land.

Those species that live on land for much of the year and only have their young in the water, often choose small pools that are only filled with water part of the year. Such pools are called temporary pools. Temporary pools, since they dry up later in the year, usually do not contain fish, which often eat amphibian eggs

THE RISE OF THE AMPHIBIANS

The oldest fossil amphibian is about 250 millions years old, but amphibians were around even before that. These animals lived when the Earth had only one large land mass that was surrounded by ocean. That land mass was called Pangaea (pan-JEE-uh). When Pangaea began to break up about 190 million years ago, the amphibians were split up, too. The land masses continued to move around the globe and split up into the continents as they are today. While these movements were taking place, the amphibians were changing and becoming new species. Some had features that made them well-suited to life in certain temperatures or certain areas. Today, the Earth holds thousands of different species.

and young. The only problem with laying eggs in a temporary pool is that the pools sometimes dry up too fast for the eggs to hatch into the tadpoles or larvae and for these to turn into land-living amphibians. When this happens, the young may die.

In each major group of amphibians, some species remain in the water for their entire lives. These are known as fully aquatic (uh-KWOT-ik) animals. The word *aquatic* means that an organism lives in the water, and the word *fully* means that it can always live there. Some caecilians from South America live in the water. Sirens and mudpuppies are types of salamanders that live in the water as eggs, larvae, and adults. As adults, both have bodies that are well-designed for swimming instead of walking on land. They have strong, flattened tails to move swiftly through the water but very tiny legs. The sirens only have two small front legs and have neither back legs nor hip bones.

Many frogs are fully aquatic. The clawed frogs and Surinam toads, for instance, live in just about any kind of freshwater, including swamps, slow streams, and ponds. They have very large and webbed hind feet, which make excellent paddles. One very unusual frog is the hairy frog. Adults of this species live on land most of the year, but the males will stay with the eggs underwater until they hatch. During this time, the male develops "hairs" all over the sides of its body. The hairs are actually thin fringes made of skin. This gives him more skin area and makes it easier for him to breathe. With his "hairs," he is able to stay underwater for days with his eggs without ever coming up for air.

Tadpoles, aquatic larvae, and some aquatic adult amphibians have lateral (LAT-eh-rul) line systems. Fishes have lateral line systems, too. The lateral line system looks like a row of stitch-like marks or dots that runs down each side of the body. Inside each mark or dot are tiny hairs that sway one way or the other with the movements of the water. When another animal swims past or enters the water nearby, the hairs lean and send a message to the amphibian's brain that it is not alone in the water. This helps amphibians to escape predators or, if they eat insects or other water-living prey, to find the next meal.

Along the ground

Many adult frogs and salamanders live on land and along the ground. Since they have to keep their skin moist, they often huddle under a rotting log, inside a crack in a rock, in piles of dead leaves, under the low-lying leaves of plants, or in some other damp place. Once in a while, a caecilian is also found snuggled between a leaf and stem in a low plant. In many cases, amphibians only move about on the ground during or after a heavy rain. Some, like the American toads, can survive under a bit drier conditions than other amphibians and hop or walk around the forest floor even on warm and dry summer days.

Above the ground

Some frogs and salamanders will venture into the trees. Animals that spend part of their lives off the ground and in plants or trees are known as arboreal (ar-BOR-ee-ul) animals. Among the salamanders, only some lungless salamanders are arboreal. One, which is known as the arboreal salamander, may crawl under tree bark or climb into tree holes to escape hot and dry weather. Many more frogs than salamanders are arboreal. Hundreds of these are called treefrogs and have sticky, wide pads on the tips of their toes to help them scramble up plants and trees. Some of the arboreal frogs live in humid forests that are

Life cycle of a salamander (Ambystoma opacum) and frog (Rana temporaria); a. and b.— adults; c.—eggs laid in water; d.— —terrestrial salamander eggs laid in a moist area on land; e, f, g, h—larval stage; i and j—juvenile stage. (Illustration by Jacqueline Mahannah. Reproduced by permission.)

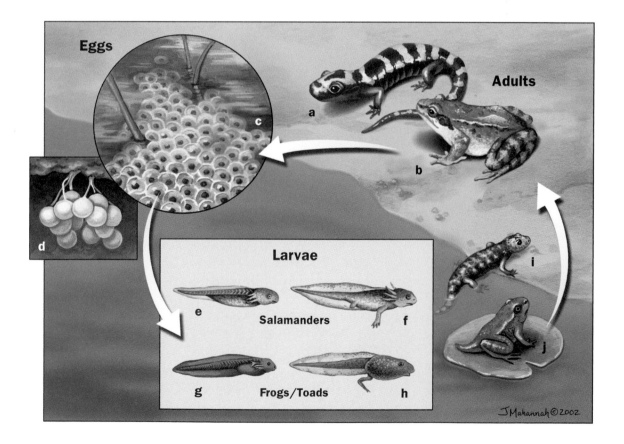

moist enough for them to sit out on leaves most of the time. Others need more moisture and find it in bromeliads (broh-MEE-lee-ads), which are plants that often grow on the sides of trees and have tube-shaped leaves that catch rainwater. There, the frogs find tiny pools where they can dip their bodies or float.

Under the soil

Since amphibians need to keep their skin moist, many of them find dampness under the soil. Animals that live underground are called fossorial (faw-SOR-ee-ul) animals. Most of the caecilians remain underground, only coming up to the surface once in a while to feed. They typically have tiny eyes and are nearly blind, although they can tell light from dark. They make their own burrows, digging headfirst into moist soil. Among the salamanders, the best-known burrowers are the mole salamanders. These salamanders, which live through much of North America, usually do not make their own burrows, instead borrowing them from mice and other small rodents. They stay inside these underground hideaways until rains wet the ground. At that time, they climb out and look for food to eat. Many of the mole salamanders, such as the blue-spotted salamander, also may live under rotting logs. The larger spotted salamander sometimes hides under rocks or deep in a damp well.

Numerous frog species, including the spadefoot toads, live underground for much of their lives. They, like many other burrowing frogs, have a hard bump that looks like the edge of a shovel blade on each of their digging feet. Some burrowing frogs do not have hard bumps on their feet. They do, however, have powerful digging legs and usually wide feet to move away the soil as they burrow.

HOW DO AMPHIBIANS MOVE?

Since amphibians may have four legs, two legs, or no legs at all, and they may spend most of their time on the ground, in the water, or in trees, they move in many different ways. Some walk or run; some hop or leap; some swim; some burrow; and some even glide through the air.

Walking and running

The land-living, or terrestrial (te-REH-stree-uhl), salamanders travel from one place to another by walking or running. They do this with their bodies very close to the ground and their upper legs held out from the body in the same position that a person takes when starting to do a push-up. Lizards, which people often confuse with salamanders, typically hold their bodies higher off the ground. The arboreal salamanders use these same movements to climb trees. Some frogs, especially those frogs with short hind legs, also get around mainly by walking. The Roraima bush toad is an example. This little toad walks slowly over the rocks where it lives. If it needs to escape quickly, it tucks in its legs so it forms a little ball and rolls off the face of the stone.

Hopping

The frogs and toads are the hoppers and leapers among the amphibians. They have two especially long ankle bones in their hind legs, as well as a long rod of bone in the hip where the jumping muscles attach. These bones give the frog's leaps added boost. They also have a strong but springy chest that can catch the frog safely as it lands on its front feet. Not all frogs and toads hop, but most do. Some, like most of the frogs in the family called true toads, have short hind legs and can only hop a short distance. Others, like most of those in the family called true frogs, have long and powerful hind legs that help them leap several times their body length. Some people even hold frog-leaping contests and bet on the frog they think will jump the farthest.

Swimming

Adult frogs swim much as they leap, shoving off with both hind feet at the same time. The frogs that are the best swimmers typically have large hind feet with webbing stretched between the toes and to the toe tips or close to the tips. Tadpoles do not have any legs until they start to turn into froglets, but they can swim by swishing their tails. Salamander larvae and the aquatic adult salamanders may or may not have tiny legs, but they all use their tails to swim. The aquatic caecilians swim much as snakes do, waving their bodies back and forth in "s" patterns to slither-swim through the water.

Burrowing

Caecilians burrow head-first into the moist soil where they live. Frogs may burrow head-first or hind feet-first. The spade-foot toads are one of the groups of frogs that dig backwards into the soil, scraping through the soil with their back feet while wriggling backward. This buries the frog deeper and deeper into the soil. The sandhill frog that lives in Australia is one of the frogs that digs head-first by paddling its front feet and making it look as if it is swimming down into the sand.

Gliding

A few of the frog species, including the flying frogs in the family known as the Asian treefrogs, can soar through the air. They do not flap their front legs or have feathers like a bird, but they do have long toes that are separated by webbing that reaches the toe tips. When they widen their toes, the feet look almost like fans. These treefrogs can leap off a tree branch high above the ground and glide safely to earth by using their fan-shaped feet to keep from falling too fast. They are also able to steer by moving their feet one way or the other.

WHAT DO AMPHIBIANS EAT?

Meat eaters

Many amphibians eat meat or are carnivorous (kar-NIH-vor-us). For most of them, their meals are insects, spiders, and other invertebrates (in-VER-teh-brehts), which are animals without backbones. Often, larger species will eat larger prey. Most caecilians eat earthworms, termites, and other invertebrates that live underground. Mexican caecilians, which may grow to 19.7 inches (500 centimeters) in length, sometimes eat other animals, such as small lizards and baby mice that crawl on top of the leaf-covered ground where the caecilians live. Most salamanders eat earthworms or small arthropods (AR-throe-pawds), which are insects and other invertebrates with jointed legs. Adult frogs also usually eat invertebrates, but if they are able to capture a larger prey and swallow it, many will. The bullfrog, which is common in much of North America, will eat anything and nearly everything from other frogs to small snakes, rodents, and even small birds.

Many amphibians hunt by ambush, which means that they stay very still and wait for a prey animal to happen by. Some amphibians hunt by foraging (FOR-ij-ing), when they crawl, hop, or swim about looking for something to eat. Many amphibians simply snap their mouths around the prey and swallow it. Some flick their tongues out to nab it and then reel their tongues and the prey back into their mouths. Many salamanders have especially long tongues.

Plant eaters

Tadpoles are usually herbivorous (urh-BIH-vor-us), which means that they eat plants. Many have beaklike mouths that scrape algae (AL-jee) and other scum from rocks and underwater plants. Some, like the tadpoles of spadefoot toads, will eat invertebrates in addition to plants.

AMPHIBIANS AS PREY

A wide variety of animals attack and eat amphibians. Birds, snakes, raccoons and other mammals, fishes, and other amphibians are their predators. Even insects, like diving beetles, can kill a tadpole. For most amphibians, the best defense against their predators is to remain still and let their camouflage colors help them stay out of sight. Frogs, in particular, are often the same color as their surroundings. Some, like the horned frogs,

Amphibian behavioral and physiological defense mechanisms; a. Marine toad (Bufo marinus) inflates its lungs and enlarges; b. Two-lined salamander (Eurycea bislineata) displays tail autotomy (tail is able to detach); c. Eleutherodactylus curtipes feigns death; d. Echinotriton andersoni protrudes its ribs; e. Bombina frog displays unken reflex. (Illustration by Jacqueline Mahannah. Reproduced by permission.)

have large and pointy heads that look much like dead leaves. Other amphibians are very brightly colored. The juvenile eastern newt, for example, is bright orange red. This newt also is very poisonous, and its bright colors advertise to predators that they are dangerous to eat.

When numerous amphibians are attacked, they will stiffen their bodies, arch their backs, and hold out their feet. This position is called the unken (OONK-en) reflex. The fire-bellied frogs use this position, which shows off their bright red, yellow, or orange undersides and the similarly colored bottoms of their feet. The colors may remind predators that these frogs have a bad-tasting poison in their skin and convince them to leave the frogs alone.

Although it is not very common, some amphibians will fight back if attacked. Adult African bullfrogs will snap at large predators, even lions or people, who come too close to the frogs or their young. Among salamanders, the large hellbenders can give a painful bite.

REPRODUCTION

In all three groups of amphibians, mating involves both males and females. The females produce the eggs, and the males make a fluid that contains microscopic cells called sperm. An egg will only develop into a baby amphibian if it mixes with sperm. This mixing is called fertilization (FUR-tih-lih-ZAY-shun). In almost all frogs, the male climbs onto the back of the female, and as she lays her eggs, he releases his fluid so that the eggs are fertilized outside. In the caecilians, the male adds his fluid to the eggs while they are still inside the female's body. Salamanders fall in between these two types of fertilization. In most salamanders, the male puts drops of his fluid along the ground, and the female follows along behind to scoop up the droplets and put them inside her body with the eggs. All amphibians either lay their eggs in the water or in a moist place where the eggs will not dry out.

Most amphibian eggs hatch into tadpoles or larvae before becoming miniature versions of the adults. Often, these eggs, tadpoles, and larvae develop in the water. In some species, the adults lay the eggs on land but near water; the eggs hatch into tadpoles or larvae that squirm into the water or scramble onto the parent's back for a ride to the water. A number of species have young that never enter the water. In many of these amphibians,

the eggs skip the tadpole or larvae stage and hatch right into miniature adults.

ACTIVITY PERIODS

Amphibians often have certain times of day or times of year when they are active. Some may even enter states of deep sleep for parts of the year when the weather is too cold or too dry.

Day and night

Most amphibians are nocturnal (nahk-TER-nuhl), which means they are active at night. Nocturnal animals hide someplace during the day. Sirens, which are the two-legged salamanders, spend their days buried in mud. Many frogs likewise stay out of sight during the day, sometimes hidden underground, in a rock crevice, or in some other hiding place, and come out at night to look for food or to mate. By being active at night instead of the daytime, these amphibians can avoid many predators that rely on their eyesight to find prey. Nights are also usually more humid than days, so the amphibians can keep their skin moist better if they are only active at night.

These aglypto frogs are engaging in a behavior known as "explosive breeding." (Photograph by Harald Schüetz. Reproduced by permission.)

Some species are diurnal (die-UR-nuhl), which means that they are active during the day. In many cases, these species have especially poisonous or bad-tasting skin that protects them from daytime predators. Many of the poison frogs of South America, for example, are diurnal. On rainy days, some of the nocturnal amphibians will come out of hiding and wander about. With the wet weather, they can keep their skin moist.

During the seasons

Many species of amphibians are active only during some times of year. Those that live in climates with a cold winter often spend the winter underground or in another sheltered spot and enter a state of deep sleep, called hibernation (high-bur-NAY-shun). The bodies of some species, like the wood frog in the family of true frogs, actually freeze in the winter, but they are able to thaw out the following spring and continue living. Many other cold-climate species become active again when the spring arrives. Salamanders in the northern United States, for instance, start to move about on land even before the snow melts. Frequently, in these species, the spring also is the time for mating.

Besides the cold-weather species, some other amphibians enter a state of deep sleep when the weather becomes too dry. For species that live in deserts or dry grasslands, such as the water-holding frog of Australia, many burrow down into the ground and wait there until the next rainy season arrives. A period of deep sleep during a dry period is known as estivation (es-tih-VAY-shun). In these species, the rainy season marks the beginning of the mating period.

Amphibians that live in warm and wet tropical areas usually are active all year long, but they often mate only on rainy days.

AMPHIBIANS AND PEOPLE

Of all the amphibians, frogs are the most familiar to people. Nearly everyone has seen a frog or heard one calling during its mating season. Because neither salamanders nor caecilians have mating calls, and both usually stay out of sight during the day, many people have seen few, if any, of these two types of animals. Frogs are also much more common pets than salamanders or caecilians. In addition, many people eat frogs and some even eat tadpoles, but few people eat caecilians or salamanders.

Scientists are interested in amphibians for many reasons. In some species, their skin poisons or other chemical compounds have been made into or studied as medicines. Scientists also use amphibians to learn how their bodies work and therefore learn more about how human bodies function. Perhaps most importantly, ecologists see amphibians as living alert systems. Since amphibians live on land and in the water, and often are very sensitive to changes in the environment, they are excellent alarms that can warn humans about problems, such as water or air pollution.

ENDANGERED AMPHIBIANS

Through the World Conservation Union, which goes by the initials IUCN, scientists keep track of how well amphibians, along with other organisms, are surviving on Earth. They separate the species into different categories based on the number of individuals in the species and anything that might make them lose or gain numbers in the future. One of the categories the IUCN uses is called Data Deficient. This category means that scientists do not have enough information to make a judgment about the threat of extinction. The number of amphibians listed as Data Deficient is quite large: 1,165 species of frogs, 62 species of salamanders, and 111 caecilians. Many of these species are rare and/or live underground or in some other hard-to-reach location where they are difficult to study.

EXTRA LEGS?

In 1995, a group of students at the Minnesota New Country School were outside hiking when they found frogs with odd legs, including extra feet. In all, half of the frogs they saw had some type of deformity. After this discovery, many other people began reporting other deformed frogs. Scientists immediately started tests and experiments to learn why the frogs were deformed. Today, many believe the deformities were the result of disease, pollution, and/or some of the sun's rays, called UV radiation.

Amphibians in danger

The IUCN lists 367 species of frogs and forty-seven species of salamanders as Critically Endangered and facing an extremely high risk of extinction in the wild; 623 frog species, 106 salamanders, and one caecilian are Endangered and facing a very high risk of extinction in the wild; 544 frogs, 86 salamander species, and three caecilians are Vulnerable and facing a high risk of extinction in the wild; and 302 frogs and fifty-nine salamanders are Near Threatened and at risk of becoming threatened with extinction in the future.

Many of these species are at risk because the places where they live or breed are disappearing or changing, perhaps as

Amphibian morphological defense mechanisms; a. Darwin's frog (Rhinoderma darwinii) uses camouflage and cryptic structure; b. Pseudotriton ruber and Notophthalmus viridescens display mimicry; c. Bufo americanus has poison parotid glands; d. Poison dart frog (Dendrobates pumilio) has warning coloration; e. Physalaemus nattereri has eye spots on its hind quarters. (Illustration by Jacqueline Mahannah. Reproduced by permission.)

people cut down trees for lumber or otherwise clear the land to put in farms, homes, or other buildings. Some of the other problems for amphibians come from air and water pollution, infection with a fungus that is killing amphibians around the world, and global warming. Global warming changes weather patterns, sometimes causing especially dry conditions in some places. Since frogs need to keep their skin moist, especially dry weather can be deadly to them.

Saving endangered amphibians

To help many of the at-risk amphibians, governments, scientific organizations, and other groups are protecting some of the areas where the animals live. These may be national parks, preserves, or other natural areas. Many local, state, and national governments have also designed laws to protect the amphibians from being hunted or collected. In a few cases, conserva-

Grzimek's Student Animal Life Resource

tionists are trying to raise amphibians in captivity and then releasing them into the wild with the hopes that they will survive, breed, and increase the size of the natural populations.

Too late to save

The efforts to protect the Earth's amphibians are important, because many species have already become extinct in recent years. An extinct species is one that is no longer in existence.

Leopard frogs with missing, deformed or extra legs started appearing near St. Albans Bay of Lake Champlain in St. Albans, Vermont. Biologists are not sure if pollution, a parasite, disease, or something else is causing the frogs to develop abnormally. Photograph AP/World Wide Photos. Reproduced by permission.

This includes two species of salamanders and thirty-two species of frogs. In addition, the IUCN lists one frog as Extinct in the Wild, which means that it is no longer alive except in captivity or through the aid of humans.

FOR MORE INFORMATION

Books:

Behler, John. *Simon and Schuster's Guide to Reptiles and Amphibians of the World.* New York: Simon and Schuster, 1989, 1997.

Clarke, Barry. *Amphibian.* New York: Dorling Kindersley, 1993.

Florian, Douglas. *Discovering Frogs.* New York: Charles Scribner's Sons, 1986.

Halliday, Tim, and Kraig Adler, eds. *The Encyclopedia of Reptiles and Amphibians (Smithsonian Handbooks).* New York: Facts On File, 1991.

Harding, J. H. *Amphibians and Reptiles of the Great Lakes Region.* Ann Arbor: The University of Michigan Press Institution Press, 1997.

Lamar, William. *The World's Most Spectacular Reptiles and Amphibians.* Tampa, FL: World Publications, 1997.

Maruska, Edward. *Amphibians: Creatures of the Land and Water.* New York: Franklin Watts, 1994.

Miller, Sara Swan. *Frogs and Toads: The Leggy Leapers.* New York: Franklin Watts, 2000.

O'Shea, Mark, and Tim Halliday. *Smithsonian Handbooks: Reptiles and Amphibians (Smithsonian Handbooks).* New York: Dorling Kindersley Publishing, 2002.

Periodicals:

Hogan, Dan, and Michele Hogan. "Freaky Frogs: Worldwide Something Weird Is Happening to Frogs." *National Geographic Explorer* (March–April 2004): 10.

Masibay, Kim Y. "Rainforest Frogs: Vanishing Act? Frog Populations Around the World Are Dying Off Mysteriously. Can Scientists Save Them—Before It's Too Late?" *Science World* (March 11, 2002): 12.

Sunquist, Fiona. "The Weird World of Frogs." *National Geographic World* (March 2002): 14.

Walters, Mark Jerome. "Spotting the Smallest Frog: As Hopes Fade for One Species, a Tiny Frog Comes into View." *Animals* (May–June 1997): 8.

Web sites:

"North American Reporting Center for Amphibian Malformations." *National Biological Information Infrastructure.* http:// frogweb.nbii.gov/narcam/index.html (accessed on May 15, 2005).

Stoddard, Tim. "Island hoppers: Sri Lankan tree frogs end game of hide-and-seek." *BU Bridge.* http://www.bu.edu/bridge/ archive/2002/10-18/frogs.htm (accessed on February 12, 2005).

Trivedi, Bijal P. "Frog Fathers Provide Transport, Piggyback Style." *National Geographic Today.* http://news.nationalgeo-graphic.com/news/2002/08/0807_020807_TVfrogs.html (accessed on February 12, 2005).

"Weird Frog Facts." *Frogland.* http://allaboutfrogs.org/weird/ weird.html (accessed on February 12, 2005).

order
CHAPTER

PHYSICAL CHARACTERISTICS

Like mammals, birds, bony fishes, reptiles, and other amphibians, frogs are vertebrates (VER-teh-brehts). A vertebrate is an animal with a spine, or backbone. Compared with all the other vertebrates, frogs are the only ones that have this combination of features:

- A wide head and large mouth
- Two big, bulging eyes
- A short body with only eight or nine bones in the spine
- Two extra bones in the ankle area that make their long legs even longer
- A long, rod-shaped bone, called a urostyle (YUR-oh-stile) in the hip area
- No tail

Most of the frogs are about 1.5 to 3.0 inches (3.5 to 7.5 centimeters) long from the tip of the snout to the end of the rump. Some are much smaller. The smallest species are the Brazilian two-toed toadlet and the Cuban Iberian rain frog, which only grow to about 0.4 inches (1 centimeter) long. These compare with the unusually large Goliath frog, which can grow to 12.6 inches (32 centimeters) long and weigh 7 pounds (3.25 kilograms).

Depending on the species, the skin on a frog may be smooth, somewhat bumpy, or covered with warts. Although many people think that all warty frogs can be called toads, only those in one family of frogs are true toads. The members of this family typically have chubby bodies, rather short hind legs, and many warts. What sets them apart from other frogs—even those that are also chubby, warty, and short-legged—is something called a Bidder's organ. A Bidder's organ is a female body part that is found inside a male toad. This tiny organ does not appear to do anything in a healthy male toad, but it does help scientists tell a true toad from all other kinds of frogs.

A great number of frogs are green, brown, gray, and other colors that look much like the background in the place they live. They also have spots, stripes, and other patterns that help them blend into their surroundings. Many of the poison frogs, among others, are not camouflaged. They have bright colors that make them very noticeable.

Most species of frogs lay eggs that hatch into tadpoles. Tadpoles are sometimes described as a sack of guts with a mouth at one end and a tail at the other. Often, the mouth on a tadpole is hard like the beak of a bird and is able to scrape bits of plants off the sides of underwater rocks. Some tadpoles instead have a fleshy mouth. These tadpoles suck in water and strain little bits of food out of it. Including their tails, tadpoles are often as long as or longer than the adult frogs. As the tadpoles change into young frogs, however, the tail slowly becomes shorter and shorter until it is gone.

GEOGRAPHIC RANGE

Frogs live in North, Central, and South America, in Europe and Asia, in Africa, and in Australia. They do not live in extremely cold areas, such as the Arctic, or on many of the islands out in the ocean. The largest number of frog species is in hot and humid tropical areas, but some make their homes in places that have all four seasons, including a cold winter. Frogs usually stay out of very dry areas, but the water-holding frog and a few others are able to survive in dry grasslands and even deserts. The majority of frogs live in valleys, lowlands, or only partway up the sides of mountains. Some, however, survive quite well high above the ground. The Pakistani toad is perhaps the highest-living frog. It makes its mountain home at 16,971 feet (5,238 meters) above sea level in the Himalayas.

HABITAT

The majority of frogs start their lives in the water as eggs, then hatch into tadpoles, which remain in the water until they turn into froglets. At that point, frogs of some species may leave the water and make their homes on land, while others may stay in the water. Some species are able to survive without ever having to even dip their feet in a puddle. Most of these frogs spend hours everyday underground or in some other moist place.

A number of frog species that live in dry areas, such as grasslands or deserts, stay underground and enter a state of deep sleep, called estivation (es-tih-VAY-shun) for much of the year. There, they wait for the rainy season and then climb back up to the ground to eat and to mate. Other frogs that live in colder places that have a frigid winter find shelter, sometimes also underground, and also enter a state of deep sleep, called hibernation (high-bur-NAY-shun). They remain in hibernation until warmer weather arrives in the spring.

DIET

Most frogs eat mainly plants when they are tadpoles and switch to a diet of mainly insects once they turn into froglets. Some tadpoles also eat little bits of dead animal matter that float down to the bottom of the water, and the tadpoles of a few species will even eat an insect or other invertebrate (in-VER-teh-breht), which is an animal without a backbone. Not all adult frogs will only eat insects. Many of the larger species will gulp down anything they can catch and swallow. Bullfrogs, which are common throughout much of North America, are one type of frog that will almost eat anything that comes within reach, including ducklings and other bullfrogs.

BEHAVIOR AND REPRODUCTION

Like other amphibians, frogs can breathe through their skin, but they can only do so if the skin is moist. Most frogs are active at night, which is when the air is more humid. Humid air helps them keep their skin moist. During the daytime, these frogs sit still in moist places, like under a rotting log, in a muddy place, underground, or in the crack of a rock. Even when frogs are active at night, they spend a good part of the time sitting still. This is how many species hunt. They remain in one place and wait for an insect or other prey animal to wander past, either grasp it with their mouths or flick out their tongues to snatch it, and swallow it whole. Most frogs have sticky tongues that attach in the front of the mouth and flip outward. Some frogs, including the poison frogs, take a more energetic approach to hunting, and hop about looking for their next meals.

FROGS IN DANGER

In the 1990s, scientists noticed that the number of frogs around the world was dropping. Some species were nearly gone, and others were already extinct. They began trying to figure out why and now believe that many things may be to blame, including air and water pollution, habitat destruction, and infection with a fungus, called chytrid (KIT-rid) fungus. They also believe that introduced species are a danger to frogs. People often add fish to streams or ponds without thinking about what will happen to the frogs that use the water, too. In many cases, fish eat frog eggs, tadpoles, and sometimes adult frogs. Just a few fish in a pond may be enough to gobble up every frog egg and tadpole for the whole season. Since most adults only live and breed for a few years, the fishes can quickly wipe out an entire frog population.

Frogs often mate based on the weather. Those that live in warm, humid places may mate any time of year but usually only do so during or after a rainstorm. Frogs that make their homes in colder climates commonly wait until the temperatures warm and the spring rains have come. For species in especially dry areas, the rainy season is the time for mating. The males of almost all frog species call during the mating season. They make the calls by sucking in and letting out air from the vocal sac, which is a piece of balloon-like skin in the throat area. Most frogs, like the spring peeper, have one vocal sac, but some species, including the wood frog, have two. The males of each species have their own calls. The calls not only attract females but sometimes tell other males to stay away and find their own mating places. In a few species, calls may not be enough, and two males may fight. Most fights are little more than wrestling matches, but in some species, like the gladiator frogs, males have sharp spines and often injure one another. In many frog species, the males call together in a group. This type of group calling is called a chorus (KOR-us). In some species, the males all call and mate over a very short time, often within a few days. Frogs that breed over such a short time are called explosive breeders.

To mate in most species, the male scrambles onto the back of a female in a piggyback position called amplexus (am-PLEK-sus) and hangs onto her. As she lays her eggs, he releases a fluid. The fluid contains microscopic cells called sperm that mix with the eggs. This mixing is called fertilization (FUR-tih-lih-ZAY-shun). Once fertilization happens, the eggs begin to develop. The tailed frogs do things a bit differently. The males have "tails," which are actually little bits of flesh they use to add their fluid to the eggs while the eggs are still inside the female's body.

Depending on the species, a frog may lay less than a dozen eggs at a time or more than a thousand. The typical female frog lays her eggs in the water, often in underwater plants, and she and the male leave the eggs alone to develop on their own. In a few species, one of the parents stays behind to watch over the eggs and sometimes stays to cares for the tadpoles, too. The typical frog egg develops in the water into a tadpole. In some species, the egg develops instead in a moist spot, and in a few species that moist spot is inside a pouch or on the back of one of the parents. A number of the frogs that have their young on land lay eggs that skip the tadpole stage and hatch right into baby frogs. In most frogs, however, the eggs hatch into tadpoles that continue growing in the water. Most tadpoles begin to change into froglets within a month or two, but some remain tadpoles for a year or more. The change from a tadpole to a froglet is called metamorphosis (meh-tuh-MOR-foh-sis). In this amazing process, the tadpole's tail becomes shorter and shorter, tiny legs sprout, and the tadpole begins to take on the shape and color of the adults. Soon a tiny froglet, often still with a little bit of the tail left, takes its first hops.

FROGS AND PEOPLE

Many people greatly enjoy the sound of frogs calling on a spring or summer night. In some places, people even gather together to listen to frog choruses. Some people eat frogs, especially frog legs, and occasionally tadpoles. Frogs are also popular as pets. Perhaps more importantly, some frogs have chemicals in their skin that are helping to treat human medical conditions. In addition, scientists are watching frog populations very closely, because frogs can help them tell whether the environment is healthy. A population that suddenly disappears from a pond, for example, may be a warning sign that the water is polluted.

CONSERVATION STATUS

The World Conservation Union (IUCN) lists thirty-two species that are Extinct, which means that they are no longer in existence; one species that is Extinct in the Wild, which means that it is no longer alive except in captivity or through the aid of humans; 367 species that are Critically Endangered and facing an extremely high risk of extinction in the wild; 623 species that are Endangered and facing a very high risk of extinction in the wild; 544 that are Vulnerable and facing a high risk of extinction in the wild; 302 that are Near Threatened and at risk of becoming threatened with extinction in the future;

and 1,165 that are Data Deficient, which means that scientists do not have enough information to make a judgment about the threat of extinction.

FOR MORE INFORMATION

Books:

Behler, John. *Simon and Schuster's Guide to Reptiles and Amphibians of the World.* New York: Simon and Schuster, Inc., 1989, 1997.

Clarke, Barry. *Amphibian.* New York: Dorling Kindersley, 1993.

Florian, Douglas. *Discovering Frogs.* New York: Charles Scribner's Sons, 1986.

Halliday, Tim, and Kraig Adler, eds. *The Encyclopedia of Reptiles and Amphibians (Smithsonian Handbooks).* New York: Facts On File, 1991.

Harding, J. H. *Amphibians and Reptiles of the Great Lakes Region.* Ann Arbor: The University of Michigan Press Institution Press, 1997.

Lamar, William. *The World's Most Spectacular Reptiles and Amphibians.* Tampa, FL: World Publications, 1997.

Maruska, Edward. *Amphibians: Creatures of the Land and Water.* New York: Franklin Watts, 1994.

Miller, Sara Swan. *Frogs and Toads: The Leggy Leapers.* New York: Franklin Watts, 2000.

O'Shea, Mark, and Tim Halliday. *Smithsonian Handbooks: Reptiles and Amphibians (Smithsonian Handbooks).* New York: Dorling Kindersley Publishing, 2002.

Periodicals:

Hogan, Dan, and Michele Hogan. "Freaky Frogs: Worldwide Something Weird Is Happening to Frogs." *National Geographic Explorer* (March–April 2004: 10).

Masibay, Kim Y. "Rainforest Frogs: Vanishing Act?" *Science World* (March 11, 2002): 12.

Sunquist, Fiona. "The Weird World of Frogs." *National Geographic World* (March 2002): 14.

Walters, Mark Jerome. "Spotting the Smallest Frog: As hopes fade for one species, a tiny frog comes into view." *Animals* (May–June 1997): 8.

Web sites:

"Anura Species Database." *LivingUnderworld.org.* http://www.livingunderworld.org/anura/families/ (accessed on May 15, 2005).

Morell, Virginia. "The Fragile World of Frogs." *National Geographic.* http://www.nationalgeographic.com/ngm/0105/feature6/index.html (accessed on February 12, 2005).

"North American Reporting Center for Amphibian Malformations." *National Biological Information Infrastructure.* http://frogweb.nbii.gov/narcam/index.html (accessed on May 15, 2005).

Stoddard, Tim. "Island hoppers: Sri Lankan tree frogs end game of hide-and-seek." *BU Bridge.* http://www.bu.edu/bridge/archive/2002/10-18/frogs.htm (accessed on February 12, 2005).

Trivedi, Bijal P. "Frog Fathers Provide Transport, Piggyback Style." *National Geographic Today.* http://news.nationalgeographic.com/news/2002/08/0807_020807_TVfrogs.html (accessed on February 12, 2005).

NEW ZEALAND FROGS

Leiopelmatidae

Class: Amphibia

Order: Anura

Family: Leiopelmatidae

Number of species: 4 species

phylum

class

subclass

order

monotypic order

suborder

▲ **family**

PHYSICAL CHARACTERISTICS

New Zealand frogs are rather small creatures that have wide heads with large eyes and round pupils, but no showing eardrums. They have little or no webbing between the toes on their front or hind feet. Their four feet also have smooth soles, a feature that sets them apart from similar species living in New Zealand, which have pads or suckers on their feet. New Zealand frogs are usually brown, but some are green or reddish brown. Most have dark brown to black patterns on their legs and backs. Lines of raised bumps on their backs and other small bulges on their bellies, legs, and/or feet hold poison. These bumps are called granular (GRAN-yoo-ler) glands. When a predator bites one of these frogs, the poison in the glands oozes out, which may cause the predator to spit out the frog, and possibly learn to leave the frogs alone in the future, too.

New Zealand frogs grow to 0.8 to 2 inches (2 to 5.1 centimeters) long from the tip of the head to the end of the rump.

GEOGRAPHIC RANGE

Although they share New Zealand with a few other species of frogs, the members of this family are the only frogs that are actually native to New Zealand. Humans introduced, or brought in, the others, which include two species of bell frogs and a brown tree frog. New Zealand frogs live on North, Maud, Great Barrier, and Stephens Islands. Conservationists in 1997 introduced one of the four species to Motuara Island, where it is surviving.

HABITAT

Most New Zealand frogs live in damp, forested areas, where they often hide during the day under rotting logs or loose stones. Some also survive among rocks and shrubs in a misty but almost treeless part of Stephens Island. Of the four species, Hochstetter's frog prefers the wettest environment, often living near streams or other bodies of water.

DIET

These small frogs eat insects and other invertebrates (in-VER-teh-britts), which are animals without backbones, that live in their habitat. Many species of frogs capture their prey by flinging out their long tongues and using them to grasp. New Zealand frogs, on the other hand, cannot stick out their tongues. Instead, a New Zealand frog must quickly lunge at a prey animal and grab it with its mouth.

BEHAVIOR AND REPRODUCTION

Most people, including the native people who have lived near them for thousands of years, are completely unaware of these quiet little frogs. New Zealand frogs make almost no noise. They may offer a soft squeak if they are roughly handled or some faint squealing sounds during the mating season. Otherwise, they remain silent and even stop moving if a person or some other possible predator comes close. These behaviors, combined with the frogs' camouflage colors and patterns, hide them from all but the most careful observers. In addition, these frogs are mostly nocturnal (nahk-TER-nuhl), which means that they are active at night. The darkness also helps to hide the frogs from sight.

Sometimes, however, predators are still able to find them. If the frogs have the chance to escape by jumping into the water, they will. They swim by kicking one leg at a time instead of kicking both hind legs together, as other frogs do. If they cannot escape a predator, three of the four species defend themselves by raising up on their four legs so they are as tall as possible and turning their bodies to face the predator. This puts

THREE RECENT EXTINCTIONS

Fossils scattered throughout New Zealand show that it once was home to many frogs—all in the family Leiopelmatidae. These frogs, which have the fitting common name of New Zealand frogs, included three species that lived on the islands until 1,000 to 2,000 years ago, when they became extinct. Today, four species from this family still exist in New Zealand, but they live in very small areas compared to the land the family once called home.

JURASSIC FROGS

Scientists are especially interested in New Zealand frogs because they have some very primitive features, including extra backbones and muscles that are designed to move tails. Since the frogs have no tails, scientists believe the tail-wagging muscles are left over from long extinct ancestors of these species. The only other living frogs with these features are frogs of the family Ascaphidae. The extra backbones are also seen in fossils from the first frogs to live on Earth. The fossils date back to about 150 million years ago, which means the frogs shared the planet with dinosaurs.

forward their largest poison glands, those located in long bumps or ridges behind each eye, so that the attacker's first chomp is a mouthful of bad-tasting poison. Hochstetter's frog does not raise up its body as a line of defense, because its poison glands are on its belly not on its back.

During mating season, most species of frogs find one another by either making loud calls, in the case of the males, or responding to those calls, as the females do. Since New Zealand frogs do not call and even lack a real voice box, scientists think that they find each other by their smells instead. The female lays five to 20 eggs, depending on the species. The developing frog is visible inside the see-through egg capsule. Hochstetter's frog lays its eggs at streamside, and the animals go through a short tadpole stage before becoming frogs. The other three species—Archey's, Hamilton's, and Maud Island frogs—all lay their eggs on land, but under rotting logs or in other moist spots. These frogs go through their tadpole stage while still inside the eggs, so the eggs hatch right into tiny frogs. The male in all three of these species stays with the eggs until they hatch, often covering them with his body. He continues to protect newly hatched young by letting them climb onto his back and legs. Male Hochstetter's frogs do not care for their young.

NEW ZEALAND FROGS AND PEOPLE

As people have developed the land in New Zealand, these frogs have had to survive in smaller and smaller areas. Strict laws are now in place to protect the frogs and the places they live.

CONSERVATION STATUS

According to the World Conservation Union (IUCN), all four species in this family are in danger. The most at-risk species is Archey's frog, listed as Critically Endangered, which means that it faces an extremely high risk of extinction in the wild. They were once much more common, but when scientists counted them in 1996 and again in 2002, they found that their numbers fell by 80 percent: four out of every five frogs had disappeared. In one population, the number of frogs went from 433 individuals to just 53. The cause of the drop was probably disease, possibly caused by a fungus. Scientists first became aware of the fungus, called chytrid (KIH-trid) fungus, in Australia and Central America in 1998 and have since blamed it for the declines of many frog species. They think an introduced species, called the Australian bell frog, brought the fungus to New Zealand and passed it on to Archey's frog in about 1998. The fungus is still a problem. When the fungus infects one of these frogs, it has trouble moving and soon becomes paralyzed.

The IUCN considers Hamilton's frog to be Endangered, which means that it faces a very high risk of extinction in the wild. The remaining two species, Maud Island and Hochstetter's frogs, are Vulnerable and face a high risk of extinction in the wild. The major threats to these species are introduced predators, including rats and ermines, which are in the weasel family, and the lizard-like tuataras. In some cases, conservationists are trying to build barriers around the frogs' habitats so the predators cannot reach them. In addition, scientists are keeping a watchful eye on these three species to see if the chytrid fungus eventually affects them, too.

Hamilton's frog (*Leiopelma hamiltoni*)

HAMILTON'S FROG
Leiopelma hamiltoni

Physical characteristics: Hamilton's frog is usually light brown with a single dark stripe running along each side of the head and through the eye. It also has a noticeable ridge running from the head down each side of the body. Its feet have no webbing between the toes. The frog grows to 2.0 inches (5.1 centimeters) long from snout to rump. Females are usually a bit larger than males.

Geographic range: One of the rarest frogs in the world, it lives in a tiny area high atop Stephens Island in New Zealand.

Habitat: Although its preferred habitat is likely moist forest, this species now survives in a damp, rocky pile that is covered mostly by grasses and shrubs.

Diet: Hamilton's frog eats insects and other invertebrates.

Behavior and reproduction: This frog, for the most part, remains out of sight during the day. Like the other New Zealand frogs, it does not call. It can, however, squeak if mishandled. Females lay five to nine eggs at a time on land. Each egg hatches into a tiny frog. The males watch over the eggs and young.

Hamilton's frogs and people: Humans rarely notice this quiet frog.

Conservation status: The IUCN considers Hamilton's frog to be Endangered, which means that it faces a very high risk of extinction in the wild. Protection efforts are under way to protect its small home area and to help it survive into the future. ■

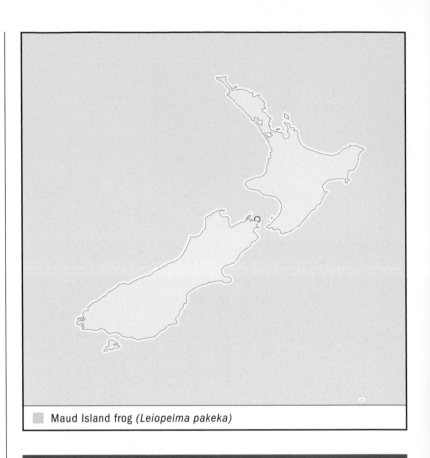

Maud Island frog (*Leiopelma pakeka*)

MAUD ISLAND FROG
Leiopelma pakeka

Physical characteristics: The Maud Island frog looks so much like Hamilton's frog that scientists thought they were the same species until 1998. At that time, they compared their DNA and found that the frogs were different enough to be separated into two species. DNA, which is inside the cells of all animals, is a chain of chemical molecules that carry the instructions for creating each species and each individual. When looking at the frogs from the outside, the biggest difference between the two species is their color: the Maud Island frog is paler, but only slightly. They both have unwebbed feet and ridges on the back, and each grows to 2.0 inches (5.1 centimeters) long from snout to rump. Females are a bit larger than males.

In 1997, conservationists gathered 300 Maud Island frogs and transplanted them to Motuara Island, where they seem to be surviving well. (Illustration by Brian Cressman. Reproduced by permission.)

Geographic range: It lives on a tiny scrap of land, measuring just 0.06 miles^2 (0.15 kilometers^2) on Maud Island in New Zealand. In 1997, conservationists gathered 300 individuals and transplanted them to Motuara Island, where the frogs seem to be surviving well.

Habitat: This frog makes its home in the forest that covers the east side of a hill on Maud Island. Although the forest reaches up the hill to about 980 feet (300 meters), the frog tends to live in the lower portion, where the slope is flatter and the climate is more moist. This species often hides among rocks and logs.

Diet: It eats insects it finds in its habitat.

Behavior and reproduction: The Maud Island frog stays out of sight during the day and comes out at night to hop slowly about and look for food. Female Maud Island frogs lay their eggs, which can number up to 20, in damp spots on the forest floor. Each male watches over his eggs until they hatch into tiny frogs. He allows the froglets to climb up his legs and onto his back.

Maud Island frogs and people: Humans rarely see this nighttime frog.

Conservation status: According to the World Conservation Union, the Maud Island frog is Vulnerable, which means that it faces a high risk of extinction in the wild. The current major threat to this species is introduced predators, including rats and ermines. Efforts are under way to keep the predators away from the frogs. Additional efforts proceed to protect and restore the frog's tiny habitat on Maud Island and to introduce the frog to a new area on Motuara Island.   ■

FOR MORE INFORMATION

Books:

Grigg, G., R. Shine, and H. Ehmann, eds. *The Biology of Australasian Frogs and Reptiles*. Chipping Norton, Australia: Surrey Beatty and Sons, 1985.

Hutching, Gerard. *The Natural World of New Zealand: An Illustrated Encyclopaedia of New Zealand's Natural Heritage*. Auckland: Penguin, 1998.

Jones, Jenny. *Hamilton's Frog*. Auckland: Heinemann Education, 1994.

Robb, Joan. *New Zealand Amphibians and Reptiles in Color*. Auckland: Collins Publishers, 1980.

Web sites:

Barnett, Shaun. "The Trouble with Frogs." *Forest and Bird Magazines*. http://www.forestandbird.org.nz/magazines/00Feb/frogs.asp (accessed on January 20, 2005).

"Frogs." Christchurch City Libraries. http://library.christchurch.org .nz/Childrens/FactSheets/Animals/Frogs.asp (accessed on January 28, 2005).

Kingsley, Danny. "Ancient Frogs Threatened by Fungus." *ABC Science Online*. http://www.abc.net.au/science/news/enviro/EnviroRepublish_ 537533.htm (accessed on January 20, 2005).

Lehtenin, R. "Leiopelmatidae." *Animal Diversity Web*. http:// animaldiversity.ummz.umich.edu/site/accounts/information/ Leiopelmatidae.html (accessed on January 20, 2005).

"Native Frog Facility to Open at Auckland Zoo." *Scoop*. http://www.scoop .co.nz/mason/stories/AK0410/S00129.htm (accessed on January 20, 2005).

"New Zealand Ecology: Living Fossils." *TerraNature*. http://www .terranature.org/living_fossils.htm (accessed on January 20, 2005).

"Welcome to the New Zealand Frog Survey (NZFS)!" University of Otago. http://www.otago.ac.nz/Zoology/frogs/#nz%20species (accessed on January 20, 2005).

family

CHAPTER

PHYSICAL CHARACTERISTICS

The tailed frogs get their name from their "tails," but only the males have them and they are not really tails at all. The tiny nub of a "tail" is really a fleshy structure that the adult male uses to mate with a female. Besides the "tails," the males and females look alike. Both have wide heads and large eyes with vertical, often diamond-shaped pupils. Unlike many other frogs, they have no round patch of an eardrum showing on the sides of the head. The skin of the tailed frog's back is covered with little warts, giving it a grainy look.

The frogs are usually shades of brown or gray, sometimes with a hint of green or red, and have darker markings, including blotches on the back and bands on all four legs. A lighter-colored patch, usually outlined with a thin, dark stripe, stretches between the eyes. Once in a while, a tailed frog may be almost completely black. The underside is pink, sometimes speckled with white. Tailed frogs have slender forelegs with no webbing on the toes and larger hind legs with well-webbed toes. Their toes, especially the outside toe on each foot, are quite wide.

Adult tailed frogs are small, growing only to 1.2 to 2.0 inches (3 to 5 centimeters) long from the tip of the snout to the end of the rump. The females are a bit bigger than the males. The tailed frog tadpole is dark gray and has a large, telltale sucker on the bottom of its broad head. Like other frogs, the tadpole has a long tail. When it begins to change into a frog, the tail shrinks until it disappears altogether. Often, people see an adult male tailed frog and believe that it is just a froglet that still has

phylum

class

subclass

order

monotypic order

suborder

family

some of its tadpole tail left. This is not correct. The fleshy nub on an adult male tailed frog is different from a tadpole tail and never disappears.

Two species of tailed frogs exist: the Rocky Mountain tailed frog and the coastal tailed frog. They look so much alike that scientists thought they were the same species until 2001 when they compared the frogs' DNA. DNA, which is inside the cells of all animals, is a chain of chemical molecules that carry the instructions for creating each species and each individual. In other words, DNA is a chemical instruction manual for "building" a frog. The DNA of the Rocky Mountain tailed frog and the coastal tailed frog were just different enough to separate them into two species.

Both of these frog species have very small lungs, compared to most other frogs, and have extra backbones. Only one other living group of frogs, the New Zealand frogs, has the same extra backbones. Scientists have found fossil frogs far in the past that had the extra bones. These date back to the dinosaur age 150 million years ago and are the oldest known frogs.

GEOGRAPHIC RANGE

Both species live in North America. The coastal tailed frog lives along the Pacific Ocean coastline from northern California in the United States into British Columbia in Canada, but not on Canada's Vancouver Island. The Rocky Mountain tailed frog makes its home in Idaho, western Montana, southeastern Washington, northeastern Oregon, and the most southeastern portion of British Columbia.

HABITAT

These frogs are found in or near clear, rocky, swift-moving streams that flow through forests. When they are in the fast current, they breathe mainly through their skin and do not have to rely on their lungs as much. Human beings get their oxygen by breathing air into the lungs. There, blood picks up the oxygen out of the air and delivers it through blood vessels to the rest of the body. Frogs can get their oxygen from the water. Water, also known as H_2O, is made up of two chemicals: hydrogen and oxygen. (The H_2 means two atoms of hydrogen are in every molecule of water, and the O means one atom of oxygen is in each molecule.) The water runs past the frog, and blood vessels near the surface of its skin take up the oxygen from the flow. This arrangement allows the frog to survive even though it has very small lungs. On land, the frogs continue to breathe through the skin, which they must keep moist, but they are also able to take up some oxygen from the air through their lungs, as people do.

DIET

Adult tailed frogs eat insects, snails, and other invertebrates (in-VER-teh-brehts), which are animals without backbones, that they find either in the water or on land nearby. Tailed frogs do not have long tongues that flip far out of their mouths to nab prey. Rather, they have short tongues that are of little use for catching passing invertebrates. They are able to capture prey by remaining still and waiting for an insect or other prey animal to come just close enough that the frog can quickly jump out and grab the insect with its mouth. Tadpoles get their food another way. Tadpoles use the strong sucker around the mouth to cling to underwater rocks and avoid being swept away by the current. While they are hanging on, they scrape up and eat bits of algae (AL-jee) with their rows of tiny teeth. Algae are tiny plantlike organisms that live in water and lack true roots, leaves, and stems.

BEHAVIOR AND REPRODUCTION

During the day, adult tailed frogs stay hidden in damp to wet spots under rocks along the streamside. At night, especially during or after a rain, they hop about on land near the stream to look for food. They still must keep their skin moist while they are out of the water, because dry skin prevents them from taking up oxygen from the air. They move about on land by hopping and in the streams by sweeping their strong hind feet as they swim through the water. When in the water, they tend to stay in areas where overhanging trees cast shadows. Newly hatched tadpoles, which are almost see-through compared to the darker, older tadpoles, remain in slower water, often in small side pools where the current is calmer. The larger tadpoles, however, brave the strong current by using their large suckers to attach tightly to rocks.

These small frogs mate in the fall. They do so quietly because male tailed frogs do not call, as the males of most other frog species do. During the breeding season, the males grow black pads on their front feet and small black bumps on their

PIGGYBACK PADS

Many male frogs, including the tailed frogs, have rough pads on the soles of their front feet that they use during mating season. In the case of the tailed frogs, the pads are black, but they can be other colors, too. Called nuptial (NUHP-shul) pads, they help the males grab hold of the female's often slippery body during mating. This grip, in which the male looks as if he is taking a piggyback ride on the female's back, is called amplexus (am-PLEK-sus). Depending on the species, the male may hold onto the female up by her forelegs, a position that is called axial (ACK-see-uhl) amplexus, while the male of other species, including the tailed frog, may hang on in front of her hind legs in a position called inguinal (ING-gwuh-nuhl) amplexus.

forelegs and along their sides. These pads and bumps help the male grab and hang onto the back of a female during mating. As in other frogs, the male tailed frog must add a fluid to the female's eggs so they will develop into tadpoles and frogs. This process is called fertilization (FUR-tih-lih-ZAY-shun). The eggs are actually fertilized by microscopic cells called sperm that float inside the male's fluid. In most frogs, the male adds his sperm-filled fluid to the eggs as the female lays them, so the mixing of the eggs and sperm cells happens outside her body. A male tailed frog, however, fertilizes the eggs differently. He swings his "tail" around, squeezes it into the hole in the female's body that she will use to lay her eggs, and releases the fluid inside her body instead of outside. The female then saves the fluid within her body until she is ready to lay her eggs the next summer. When she does lay them, her eggs are already fertilized. The type of fertilization that happens inside the female's body is called internal (in-TER-nuhl) fertilization. The other type of fertilization, which happens outside the body and is used by most other species of frogs, is called external (eks-TER-nuhl) fertilization.

A female tailed frog can lay 35 to 100 eggs at a time. She lays her eggs underwater, sticking them under rocks and usually in an area of the stream where the current is slower, so the eggs are not swept away downstream. The eggs hatch about six weeks later into small, colorless tadpoles, which soon develop the mouth suction cups and grow into larger, dark-colored tadpoles. They may remain tadpoles for five to seven years before they finally turn into small froglets. They usually switch from tadpole to froglet in the spring or summer. The froglets may need another 3 to 8 years before they are adults themselves. This is unusual. Most other species of frogs go from egg to tadpole to froglet to adult frog in a shorter amount of time, often within a single year. The tailed frogs not only take a much longer time to develop, but they also stick around longer overall. They often live in the wild to the ripe old age of 15 or

20 years, making them some of the longest-living frogs in the world. Through their long lives, tailed frogs remain near the spot in the stream where they were born.

TAILED FROGS AND PEOPLE

People are often not aware of these quiet, little nighttime frogs, and believe they are very rare. However, they are actually quite plentiful in their habitat.

CONSERVATION STATUS

Neither species is considered to be at risk. Conservationists continue to keep watch over the frogs, however, because they must have clean and clear streams to survive. Human activity, such as logging or nearby housing development, can cause dirt and other things to wash into the frogs' streams, making the water too muddy or too polluted for the frogs to survive. Organizations in Canada, in particular, have begun protecting the habitat of this frog.

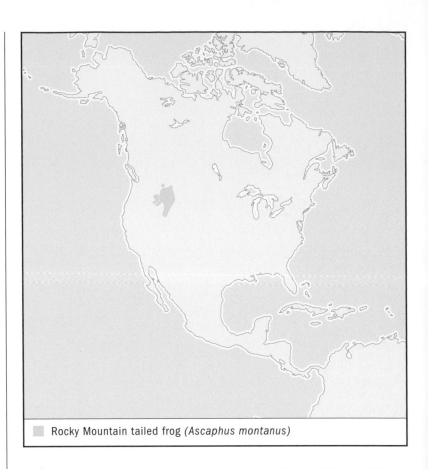

Rocky Mountain tailed frog (*Ascaphus montanus*)

ROCKY MOUNTAIN TAILED FROG
Ascaphus montanus

Physical characteristics: The Rocky Mountain tailed frog is a medium-sized brown to brownish black, sometimes gray, frog with tiny black specks. A lighter brown patch spreads between the large eyes, often dipping down toward the rounded snout. Its belly is pink. The male has a small nub of a "tail," which is actually not a real tail at all. It looks almost identical to the coastal tailed frog, except that the Rocky Mountain species has a bit more webbing between the toes of its hind feet and its tadpoles do not have the white-spotted tail tip that many of the coastal species' tadpoles do. Adults of both the Rocky Mountain tailed frog and the coastal species usually grow to 1.2 to 2.0 inches (30 to 50 millimeters) long from snout to rump.

Geographic range: This species is found in the northwestern United States, including Idaho, Montana, Oregon, and Washington and in British Columbia in Canada.

Habitat: Rocky Mountain tailed frogs live in mountain forests near and often in small, clear, rocky-bottomed streams with fast currents.

Diet: They eat insects and other invertebrates they catch in the water or on land nearby. They look for food at night. Tadpoles are vegetarians and use their small teeth to scrape algae (AL-jee), or microscopic plantlike organisms, off underwater rocks.

Behavior and reproduction: Active mainly at night, they spend their days hidden under rocks along the shoreline. They mate in the fall, and each female lays 45 to 75 eggs in the water the following summer. The eggs hatch into tadpoles, which may remain in that state for up to five years. Finally, the tadpoles turn into froglets, and another seven or eight years later, they are adults. In the wild, the frogs may live to be 15 to 20 years old.

Rocky Mountain tailed frogs and people: Scientists find both species of tailed frogs interesting because they have some features of the earliest known frogs that hopped the Earth at the time of the dinosaurs, and they mate differently from most other frogs alive today.

Conservation status: The Rocky Mountain tailed frog is not considered to be at risk. The Committee on the Status of Endangered Wildlife in Canada, however, lists it as Endangered, which means that it may soon disappear. Organizations in British Columbia have begun protecting the frog's habitat, including land in the Wycliffe Wildlife Corridor in the Kootenay region of British Columbia. ∎

FOR MORE INFORMATION

Books:

Corkran, Charlotte. *Amphibians of Oregon, Washington, and British Columbia.* Auburn, WA: Lone Pine Publishing, 1996.

Nussbaum, R. A., E. D. Brodie, and R. M. Storm. *Amphibians and Reptiles of the Pacific Northwest.* Moscow: University of Idaho Press, 1983.

Stebbins, Robert C. *A Field Guide to Western Reptiles and Amphibians (Peterson Field Guide Series).* Boston: Houghton Mifflin, 2003.

Wright, A. H., and A. A. Wright. *Handbook of Frogs and Toads of the United States and Canada.* Ithaca, NY: Comstock, 1949.

Web sites:

"I Only Have Eyes for You." *All About Frogs.* http://allaboutfrogs.org/weird/general/eyes.html (accessed on February 7, 2005).

Mierzwa, Ken. "In Search of Tailed Frogs." *Ken Mierzwa.* http://kmier.net/ecology/tailed.html (accessed on January 31, 2005).

"Rocky Mountain Tailed Frog." *The Land Conservancy.* http://www.conservancy.bc.ca/sectioncontent.php?sectionid=55&pageid=380 (accessed on January 31, 2005).

"Tailed Frog." *Yahooligans Animals.* http://yahooligans.yahoo.com/content/animals/species/4281.html (accessed on January 31, 2005).

Thompson, Don. "Frogs Provide Clues to Calif. Environment." *Kansas City Star* (Monday, November 10, 2003). http://www.kansascity.com/mld/kansascity/news/nation/7227129.htmMon, Nov. 10, 2003 (accessed on February 7, 2005).

Class: Amphibia

Order: Anura

Family: Bombinatoridae

Number of species: 10 species

family

CHAPTER

PHYSICAL CHARACTERISTICS

Fire-bellied toads are best known for the striking red, or-ange, or yellow colors that many species have on their throats, bellies, and even the undersides of the forelegs. They are named for these flame-like colors, which have black or gray spots, blotches, and patterns running through them. When seen from the top, the frogs show no hint of the bright colors underneath, and the brown, gray, and/or green of their backs and heads blend in with the environment. Some have patterns on their backs, but these also camouflage the frog rather than make it more noticeable. The barbourulas are also colored in muddy greens and browns, but they do not have the flashy undersides of the fire-bellied toads.

Members of this family have skin on their backs that is cov-ered with warts and sometimes with pointy warts that look like tiny spikes. The belly skin, in contrast, is much smoother and in most cases has no warts at all. The head has a rounded snout and two large eyes with triangular pupils, and the sides of the head do not have the round eardrums, or tympanums (tim-PAN-umz) seen in many other frogs.

The frogs are small- to medium-sized. Adults grow from 1.6 to 3.9 inches (4 to 10 centimeters) long from the tip of the snout to the rump. Males and females look alike, except that the males have leathery pads on their front feet. The males use these pads to clutch onto the females during the mating season.

Even though the fire-bellied toads and barbourulas are often listed as being in their own family, some people prefer to group

phylum

class

subclass

order

monotypic order

suborder

▲ **family**

them into another family that also contains the midwife toads and painted frogs. Other scientists like to split them into still different arrangements. Scientists are not sure which is best, but most lean toward the family as it is described here.

GEOGRAPHIC RANGE

Fire-bellied toads and barbourulas can be found in Europe and Asia, including parts of eastern and western Russia, Ukraine, Turkey, China, and Korea. Some species also live farther south in Vietnam, Borneo, and the Philippines.

HABITAT

The members of this family live mostly in the water. The fire-bellied toads prefer marshy areas, or small, often shallow ponds, where the water has little if any current. The barbourulas, on the other hand, like the faster-moving water of mountain streams and small pools of water that have plenty of rocks to provide hiding places.

DIET

Adults generally eat invertebrates (in-VER-teh-brehts), which are animals without backbones. These can include worms and snails, as well as beetles and other insects. The tadpoles of many species will eat insects, too, but usually fill their stomachs mostly with algae (AL-jee), plants, and fungi. Unlike many other types of frogs and toads, the members of this family do not have tongues they can flip out of their mouths to capture prey. Instead, they must lunge at prey and grab their meals with their mouths. This means that a fire-bellied toad, for example, must get close to its prey so it can leap and catch the insect before it can run or fly away. The camouflage pattern on the toad's back helps to hide it from prey and makes this type of hunting more successful.

BEHAVIOR AND REPRODUCTION

The fire-bellied toads are best known for the rather unusual way they defend themselves. The frogs have glands in the warts down their backs that can release a bad-tasting, white and foamy ooze that is also slightly poisonous. When the frog feels threatened, possibly by a predator that comes too close, it flips over, arches its back, stretches out its back legs, and reaches its forelegs up. Sometimes, the frog stays on its belly, but arches its back and spreads its legs. Both of these unusual displays show off the frog's bright red, orange, or yellow underside to the predator. Scientists call this odd back bend an unken (OONK-en) reflex. The unken reflex and the colors it displays remind the predator that this frog does not make a good snack. Despite the frog's best efforts, the defense tactic is not always successful, and many of these frogs become meals for attackers. For example, a shorebird known as a night heron may get as much as one-quarter of its diet from fire-bellied toads.

The two main types of frogs in this family—the fire-bellied toads and the barbourulas—lead very different lives. The fire-bellied toads are very active during the day, often hopping about on land in open areas, like meadows. Compared to the fire-bellied toads, the barbourulas are very shy. These frogs stay out of sight, usually hiding among rocks in the water. When barbourulas do wander onto land, their gray and brown backs help them blend into the colors of this habitat, too. This camouflage, their secretive behavior, and the small numbers of this species that exist have made barbourulas difficult to study, and scientists still know little about them.

The mating season for many of the fire-bellied toads starts in late spring and continues into the middle of summer, and some may breed two or three times a year. Unlike the males of other types of frogs, which call only during certain times of the day, male fire-bellied frogs sing at any time, even though they only mate with the females in the evening hours. Males mate with females by grabbing onto their back so they look as if they are riding them piggyback. This puts the male in the right position to fertilize (FUR-teh-lyze) her eggs as she releases them. During the mating season, a male will sometimes mistakenly grab onto a second male instead of a female. The second male frantically tries to squirm away, sometimes making a croaking squeal, known as a release call. People sometimes use this mating behavior as a quick way to tell the males from the females: During the mating season, those toads that climb onto the backs of others are likely to be males, and those who do not try to squirm away when another

WARNING STRETCH

The fire-bellied toads warn predators to stay away by bending up their bodies to show off their brightly colored undersides. The bright colors are an advertisement to the predators that the frog has a nasty taste. Many other bad-flavored frogs and salamanders also bend in this way. Scientists call this type of strange stretch an unken reflex, because unken is the German word for fire-bellied toad. A reflex is an automatic action. People have reflexes, too, such as blinking or twitching at sudden noises.

PREDATOR LEARNING

The fire-bellied toads use their colors to advertise to predators that they taste bad. This can only work, however, if the predators learn what the colors mean. How does a predator learn? When a young predator finds one of these frogs for the first time, it only sees what it thinks is an easy meal. When it takes the frog into its mouth, however, the frog oozes an unpleasant-tasting poison from its skin, and the surprised predator quickly spits it out. Sometimes the frog dies from the attack, but often it survives. In either case, the predator has learned a lesson to stay away from these frogs and anything that looks like them. This is why many poisonous animals have bright colors, especially red. Scientists call such warning colors aposematic (ay-POE-sem-AT-ik) coloration.

grips them are likely females. Just because a toad tries to get away does not necessarily mean that it is a male, however, because females who are not ready to mate will also try to escape the clutch of a male toad.

Each female can lay up to 200 eggs a year, although many lay only a few to a couple of dozen at a time. She usually drops them in the water, either on underwater plants or down on the bottom. Some frogs lay their eggs in permanent bodies of water, like streams or ponds that never dry up, but others lay their eggs in temporary pools of water that disappear in dry summer months. In about a week, sometimes longer, the eggs hatch into tadpoles. In another six weeks or so, the tadpoles turn into baby frogs. The timing is very important to those that are born in temporary pools of water. If they cannot change into toadlets before the water disappears, they may dry up and die.

The female barbourula is a bit different than the fire-bellied toad. She lays her eggs—about 80 large eggs at a time—beneath underwater stones. Little more about this species's reproduction is known.

FIRE-BELLIED TOADS, BARBOURULAS, AND PEOPLE

People often buy and sell fire-bellied toads as pets, partly for their beautiful coloration, partly for their display of the unken reflex, and partly because they are quite easy to keep. Many of these frogs can live more than ten years in captivity. Sometimes pet owners find that the flashy colors on a pet fire-bellied toad's underside fades, but they can brighten up the belly again if they feed the toad the right types of foods. The species in this family also sometimes wind up in laboratories where scientists study how they develop from eggs to adults or learn how the animals' bodies work.

CONSERVATION STATUS

Half of the ten species in this family are at risk, according to the World Conservation Union (IUCN). Four are Vulnerable, which means they face a high risk of extinction in the wild. These are the Philippine barbourula, the large-spined bell toad (also known as the Guangxi fire-bellied toad), the Lichuan bell toad, and the small-webbed bell toad (also known as the Hubei fire-bellied toad). The biggest threats to these frogs include pollution, habitat destruction, and collection for the pet trade. In addition, some are extremely rare. The large-spined bell toad, for example, is so uncommon that scientists have only found a few individuals and only in a small part of China. Fortunately, most of this area is protected inside a national nature reserve. Likewise, the Lichuan bell toad only appears to live in ten locations inside two Chinese provinces, and the habitat in many of these areas is being destroyed as new farms and homes move in. At least one of these populations, which makes its home inside a nature reserve, is protected.

The fifth of the five at-risk species is the Bornean flat-headed frog. This species is Endangered and faces a very high risk of extinction in the wild. The Bornean flat-headed frog lives in a single, tiny area that measures less than 300 miles by 300 miles (500 kilometers^2), and scientists know about it from just two individuals collected from forest rivers. Unfortunately, human activity near the rivers, including illegal gold mining, is making the rivers muddy and polluted, which may hurt the frogs that still live there.

Although the other five species in this family are not listed as being at risk, scientists are watching them closely because some groups of these frogs are disappearing. Human development in the habitat of the fire-bellied toad is wiping out entire populations of this animal.

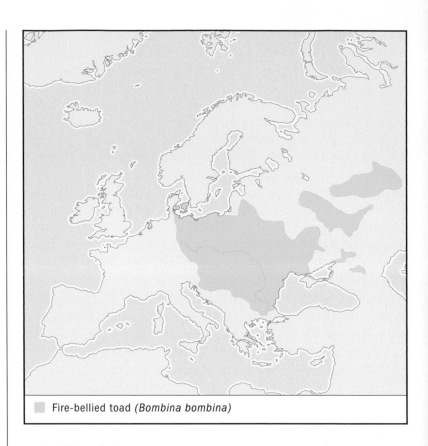

Fire-bellied toad *(Bombina bombina)*

FIRE-BELLIED TOAD
Bombina bombina

Physical characteristics: When seen from above, fire-bellied toads (also known as European fire-bellied toads) are usually dark gray or black with large black markings. When they live in places with green, leafy areas, they typically have dazzling lime-colored backs that are decorated with black spots. In both cases, their bellies are the same colors: red or orange with big black areas and small white dots. Sometimes, individuals have much more black on their bellies than red or orange. The fire-bellied toads have a rounded snout and eyes with a triangular pupil, but they do not have a flat, circular eardrum showing on each side of the head, as many other frogs do. The warts on their backs are rather tall with rounded tips. Their front feet do not have webs, but the hind feet do. Fire-bellied toads usually grow to about 1.6 inches (4 centimeters) long from snout to rump but occasionally can reach

Its bright belly colors have helped to make the fire-bellied toad very popular in the pet trade. (Photograph by Harald Schüetz. Reproduced by permission.)

2 inches (5 centimeters) long. Males and females look similar, except that the male has a slightly bigger head. In addition, the males develop pads on two of the toes on each front foot and on the inside of the forelegs throughout the breeding season. A male uses these pads to help him cling to the female during mating.

Geographic range: Fire-bellied toads live in central and eastern Europe, including Denmark, Austria, Germany, Poland, Greece, Turkey, and other nations. Sweden and the United Kingdom are home to some fire-bellied toads, but the toads did not get to these countries on their own. Rather, people probably brought them into the countries and released them. When a frog comes to a new place in this manner, it is said to be introduced. Sometimes, people introduce new species on purpose, perhaps thinking that they would be good additions to the area. Other times, people set free their old pets. In many cases, these pets die, but sometimes they do quite well and begin breeding. Overall, however, conservationists warn people not to introduce new species, because they may hurt the other species that are already there, perhaps by eating their food or by bringing in new and dangerous diseases.

Habitat: Fire-bellied toads live in just about any watering hole they can find. Some populations, especially those in northern areas, prefer clean waters, but those in more southern areas can survive in somewhat polluted waters. These may include lakes and ponds, rivers and streams with slow currents, marshes, and small pools of water, sometimes located in forests and sometimes in more open habitats. The toads do not live high up in the mountains, as some other members of this family do. They spend most of their time either in the water or on land near the water's edge. Summer weather can dry up the small pools of water where some of the toads live, but they are able to survive by crawling into the wet, muddy gaps that remain.

Diet: Adult fire-bellied toads are mainly insect-eaters, often gobbling up mosquitoes. They will also eat many other land insects, like beetles, ants, and flies, as well as water-living insects and other invertebrates. The tadpoles eat a few insects they find in the water, but they are mostly vegetarian and eat algae and plants.

Behavior and reproduction: These frogs are active during the daytime and spend the warm, sunlit hours swimming or hopping about on shore looking for things to eat. They are more sluggish when the temperature drops below about 60°F (15°C) and often remain hidden until the weather warms up again. On warm, humid nights, they will wander farther away from their watering holes to find food. In the water, they can usually escape predators by taking a quick, deep dive. On land, these frogs have back colors that blend into the environment. When a predator does see one and comes too close, this toad will arch its back, displaying the unken reflex, to show off its bright belly-side colors.

Once the weather begins to cool off in the fall, usually September or October, but sometimes as late as November, the fire-bellied toads begin their hibernation (high-bur-NAY-shun), which is a state of deep sleep. To survive the cold of winter, the toads bury themselves in the mud either on land or underwater on the bottom of their watering holes. Hibernation usually lasts from about October to April. In May, after they wake up and become active again, the males start calling. Although they may call during the day, they begin to call even more as the sun sets. They flatten out their bodies and call from their watery homes, sometimes with their heads above the water's surface and sometimes from underwater. To make the call, the male blows up a single vocal sac that looks like a bubble under his chin when it is inflated. When the male is not calling, the vocal sac shrinks back down and is not noticeable. The call is somewhat like a chicken's cluck. During mating, the male climbs onto the female's back and grips her in front of her hind legs. His front foot pads help him to hang on.

Each year, females can lay 80 to 300 eggs, which they lay in small groups. The eggs hatch into tadpoles about one to two weeks later, and the tadpoles turn into toadlets between July and September, but always before the next hibernation. Although they now have legs, the toadlets stay in the water for this first year. When they reach about 2 to 4 years old, they are adults and ready to become parents themselves. In the wild, fire-bellied toads can live to be about 12 years old, but in captivity they sometimes reach as much as 30 years old.

Sometimes, this species of toad will mate with yellow-bellied toads and have young. These young are called hybrids (HIGH-brihdz). Scientists have compared these hybrids to young that have parents of the same species and found that the hybrid eggs and tadpoles are ten times more likely to die before they reach three weeks old.

Fire-bellied toads and people: Its bright belly colors have helped to make this toad very popular in the pet trade.

Conservation status: This species is not considered to be at risk.   ■

Oriental fire-bellied toad *(Bombina orientalis)*

ORIENTAL FIRE-BELLIED TOAD
Bombina orientalis

Physical characteristics: Also known as an Oriental bell toad, the Oriental fire-bellied toad has a bright red to orange underside that is marked with large, dark blotches. Its back is brownish to greenish gray or bright green, usually has black and shiny spots, and is covered with pointy warts. Each of the two large eyes on its head, which is colored like the back, has a triangular pupil. Some people think the pupil looks more like a heart than a triangle. The front and back toes look as if their tips were dipped in bright orange or yellow paint. The front toes have no webbing between them, but the back toes are webbed.

Oriental fire-bellied toads usually grow to about 1.5 to 2 inches (3.8 to 5 centimeters) long from the tip of their snout to the end of the rump. Males and females look alike, except that males have slightly thicker forelegs. In addition, during breeding season, the males develop black pads on their front legs and toes. The male uses these pads, which are called nuptial (NUHP-shul) pads, to grip onto the female during mating.

Geographic range: The Oriental fire-bellied toad lives in Korea, on two Japanese islands called Tsushima and Kyushu, in northeastern China, and in parts of nearby Russia.

Habitat: Oriental fire-bellied toads usually are found in or near ponds, lakes, swamps, and slow-moving streams. They may also be found in ditches and other temporary ponds, which typically dry up during the summer. These water bodies may be in forests or meadows.

Diet: Young tadpoles are vegetarians but begin to eat insects as they grow larger. Once they become toadlets, they switch to a diet of small invertebrates. The adults eat beetles, ants, flies, and other insects that they find on land or in the water. They also eat worms and snails.

Behavior and reproduction: Like many other members of this family, Oriental fire-bellied toads display their brightly colored underside as a way to scare off predators. Often, this toad will remain on its belly, lift its legs, and stretch its forelegs over its head to provide a good look at its throat and belly colors. Sometimes, it will flip over onto its back while holding out its forelegs, a display that shows off its underside even more. It also releases a bad-tasting poison from its warts. The combination of poison and the display helps the toad avoid becoming a predator's next meal.

These toads are more active when temperatures are higher and the weather is not too dry. On these warm days, they will hop about in search of food. During especially dry spells in the summer, they sometimes take shelter under rocks or logs until a rain wets the land again. When the weather cools, usually in October, they find shelter either on the bottom of a stream or on land and hibernate for as long as seven or eight months. When they take their winter's sleep on land, they usually find a hiding spot under a pile of leaves or stones or inside a dead and rotting log or tree stump. Sometimes, up to six of these toads will spend the winter huddled together.

When the toads come out of hibernation in the spring, the males float on the surface of the water and start making their mating call. Depending on how close a person is to the calling toads, the mating call may sound like a duck quacking or more like a small bell. Males and females continue to mate throughout the summer. The female lays up to 250 large eggs a year, but only about six to 30 at a time, and places them beneath underwater rocks. Within one to two weeks, sometimes longer, the eggs hatch into tadpoles. The tadpoles change into toadlets in about two months and before hibernation. Overall, the Oriental fire-bellied toads can grow to a ripe old age. In the wild, they may live for as long as 20 years.

Oriental fire-bellied toads and people: Many people keep this toad as a pet.

Conservation status: This species is not considered to be at risk.   ■

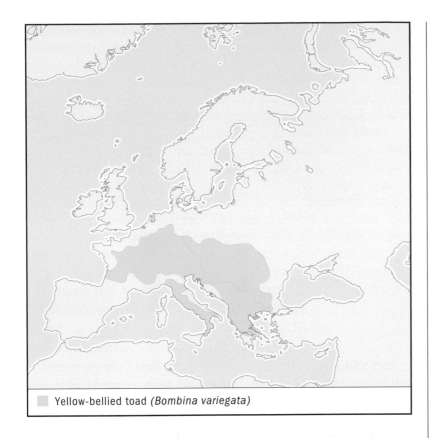

Yellow-bellied toad (*Bombina variegata*)

YELLOW-BELLIED TOAD
Bombina variegata

Physical characteristics: The yellow-bellied toad is most known for its bright yellow to yellow-orange underside, which is marked with black. The amount of black differs from individual to individual. Some may have an almost completely black belly, and others may be almost completely yellow. From a top view, however, this toad is olive-green with black speckles. These colors and the pattern on the head and back match the colors and pattern of the toad's habitat and help to hide it from predators. Compared to other members of this family, it has more warts, and its belly even has a few. This toad's warts are also different from other species because those on the back are very pointy and almost make the toad look as if it is covered with small spines. The tips of its front and back toes are yellow or yellow-orange like the belly. This species can grow to about 2 inches (5 centimeters) long

The yellow-bellied toad is most known for its bright yellow to yellow-orange underside, which is marked with black. The amount of black differs from individual to individual. Some may have an almost completely black belly, and others may be almost completely yellow. (Photograph by Harald Schüetz. Reproduced by permission.)

from snout to rump. The males and females look much alike, except that the males have pads on their front toes. During the breeding season, the males also develop pads on their forelegs. They use the pads to hold onto the female's back during mating.

Geographic range: Yellow-bellied toads live throughout much of central and southern Europe, including Austria, Greece, Hungary, Italy, Switzerland, the United Kingdom, and many other countries.

Habitat: These toads live in ponds, lakes, slow- and fast-moving streams and rivers, and pools of water in the hills and on mountainsides. They also do well near humans and can even survive in very polluted waters that would kill other types of frogs. They also spend much of their time on land in forests and/or meadows. In many places, this toad is quite common, and a person can see several toads within three feet (91 centimeters) of each other.

Diet: Unlike many other members of this family, the adult yellow-bellied toad finds almost all of its food on land. Its diet is made up of beetles, flies, ants, spiders, and other invertebrates.

Behavior and reproduction: This toad likes warmer weather and is most active during the daytime. Its schedule on a typical warm day includes time spent looking for food to eat and time resting in the water or sunbathing on land. Many cold-blooded animals, including frogs, warm themselves by such sunbathing, or basking. Like the other fire-bellied toads, the yellow-bellied toad will display the unken reflex when threatened. When the weather cools in October, it leaves the water and begins its hibernation in underground burrows or holes beneath rocks. When it awakens again the next spring, the males begin calling. Those higher in the mountains awaken last because the weather stays cold longer.

When the males and females come together, a male will climb onto a female's back and hang on just in front of her hind legs. Mating can continue off and on throughout the summer, even lasting until August. Often, a heavy rain will trigger many toads to mate at once. The female lays 45 to 100 eggs over the entire summer, but only about two dozen at a time. The eggs hatch 12 days later into tiny tadpoles. Some of the tadpoles turn into toadlets before the fall hibernation, but others wait until the following spring to make the change.

Yellow-bellied toads and people: Some people keep these toads as pets, although they are not as popular as some other species. The poison from the toad's skin, although it is not especially strong, can cause some stinging to humans who handle them.

Conservation status: This species is not considered to be at risk, but it may still be in some danger. More than a dozen populations of this toad have disappeared from the Ukraine alone, and others may soon vanish as people continue to move into and destroy their habitat. ■

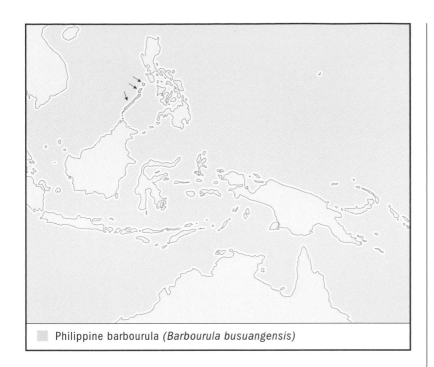

Philippine barbourula (*Barbourula busuangensis*)

PHILIPPINE BARBOURULA
Barbourula busuangensis

Physical characteristics: The Philippine barbourula is also known as the Busuanga jungle toad, the Philippine discoglossid frog, and the Philippine flat-headed frog. It is larger than any of the fire-bellied toads and typically can grow to about 3 inches (7.6 centimeters) long from its rounded snout to its rump. Like the other barbourula species, the Philippine barbourula has camouflage colors and patterns. Its back is drab brown or greenish brown with dark markings, a combination that hides the frog against the background of its water habitat. It has large eyes and a rounded snout. Both its front and back toes are webbed, which allows its feet to work like paddles as it swims through the water. Its hind legs, which are much larger and more powerful than its front legs, also give it swimming power.

Geographic range: Three western Philippine islands, called Busuanga, Culion, and Palawan, are home to this species.

Habitat: A fast-flowing, clean and clear, rocky or stony mountain stream or river is the best place to find one of these frogs. Within the

Philippine barbourulas spend much of their time floating at the top of the water, but people rarely see them because the frogs frighten easily and quickly dive out of sight to hide underneath stones or inside cracks in rocks, especially near the shoreline. (Photograph © Rafe M. Brown. Reproduced by permission.)

three Philippine islands where this species lives, it is split into small populations that are often separated quite a distance from one another.

Diet: Scientists suspect that these frogs mainly eat insects that they find in the water, although they may sometimes venture onto land to find a meal. More studies are needed to learn about their diet.

Behavior and reproduction: Philippine barbourulas spend much of their time floating at the top of the water, but people rarely see them because the frogs frighten easily and quickly dive out of sight to hide underneath stones or inside cracks in rocks, especially near the shoreline. The females even lay their large eggs beneath underwater stones. They may lay as many as 80 eggs, which possibly skip the tadpole stage and develop right into froglets. Additional studies are needed to provide more information about this secretive species.

Philippine barbourulas and people: People rarely see this species.

Conservation status: According to the World Conservation Union (IUCN), this species is Vulnerable, which means that it faces a high risk of extinction in the wild. Part of the reason the species are at risk is that people continue to damage the frogs' habitat by cutting down trees and/or by polluting the streams and rivers through such activities as mining and farming. Some people also collect these rare frogs to sell as pets. Many of the frogs on Palawan are safe from these dangers, because they live in rainforest that has been set aside as protected land. ■

FOR MORE INFORMATION

Books:

Arnold, E. Nicholas. *Reptiles and Amphibians of Europe (Princeton Field Guides)*. Princeton, NJ: Princeton University Press, 2003.

Arnold, E. N., J. A. Burton, and D. W. Ovenden. *Reptiles and Amphibians of Britain & Europe (Collins Field Guide)*. London: HarperCollins Publishing Limited, 1999.

Duellman, William E., and Linda Trueb. *Biology of Amphibians*. Baltimore: Johns Hopkins University Press, 1994.

Garcia Paris, Mario. *Los Anfibios de España*. Madrid: Ministerio de Agricultura, Pesca y Alimentación, 1985.

Gasc, Jean-Pierre, A. Cabela, J. Crnobrnja-Isailovic, et al., eds. *Atlas of Amphibians and Reptiles in Europe*. Paris: Societas Europaea Herpetologica and Muséum National d'Histoire Naturelle, 1997.

Herrmann, Hans-Joachim. *Terrarien Atlas*. Vol. 1, *Kulturgeschichte, Biologie, und Terrarienhaltung von Amphibien, Schleichenlurche, Schwanzlurche, Froschlurche*. Melle, Germany: Mergus Verlag, 2001.

Miller, Sara Swan. "Fire-Bellied Toads." *Frogs and Toads: The Leggy Leapers*. New York: Franklin Watts, 2000.

Zug, George R., Laurie J. Vitt, and Janalee P. Caldwell. *Herpetology: An Introductory Biology of Amphibians and Reptiles*. 2nd edition. San Diego: Academic Press, 2001.

Web sites:

"Fire-Bellied Toad." *The Sacramento Zoological Society.* www.saczoo.com/1_about/_animals/fact_sheets/firebellied_toad2.pdf (accessed on February 6, 2005).

"The Oriental Fire-Bellied Toad." *Utah's Hogle Zoo.* http://hoglezoo.org/animals/view.php?id=201 (accessed on February 6, 2005).

"Frogs: A Chorus of Colors." *American Museum of Natural History.* http://www.amnh.org/exhibitions/frogs/featured/flashers.php (accessed on February 6, 2005).

family

PHYSICAL CHARACTERISTICS

Midwife toads and painted frogs are medium-sized frogs that reach about 1.6 to 3 inches (40 to 75 millimeters) long from the snout to the rump. From the outside, the four species of midwife toads look quite different compared to the six painted frog species. The midwife toads have the typical pudgy-looking, warty body and rounded snout of a toad. The painted frogs, on the other hand, look much like the average frog with a trimmer body and a snout that narrows down almost to a point. Sometimes, the painted frogs are quite warty, but even so, they look more like a frog that happens to have warts than like a toad.

The two groups in this family do share several characteristics. Their bodies sit low to the ground, which gives them a squat look. Most of the midwife toads and the painted frogs have warts that are small but noticeable. Some, such as the Iberian midwife toads, even have warts on their eyelids. Both have a thick, disk-shaped tongue that resembles a small, round saucer instead of the long, thin tongue of most other species of frogs. They have large eyes, which may have vertical pupils that look like top-to-bottom slits, or somewhat heart-shaped pupils that are wider at the top than at the bottom.

The skeletons of the midwife toads and painted frogs also have some similar features. For example, the adults have just three ribs. Frogs, including the members of this family, have small, spiky ribs that attach to the backbone but not to the breastbone. Humans, on the other hand, have a full rib cage that is attached to the breastbone in the front and the backbone, or spine, in the back. Different species of frogs have different numbers of ribs, and they are attached to different places in the backbone. The midwife toads and painted frogs have three ribs attached to the second, third, and fourth bones in the spine (counted from the neck down).

The color of these frogs varies from species to species. Many have gray, brown, and black patterns that blend into the background. The midwife toads typically have reddish spots on the tops of their warts, which sometimes form noticeable rows down each side of the body. They are often a lighter color, sometimes white, on the underside. Many painted frogs have obvious dark bands on all four legs and spots and blotches on the back. The now-extinct Hula painted frog had an unusual dark belly that was speckled with white. Its scientific species name is *nigriventer*, which means a dark underside.

In some cases, members of the same species in this family look quite different. The Corsican painted frog is one such frog. In this species, some individuals are all mostly one color, usually a shade of brown or dark gray, but others are covered with obvious dark spots. In both the midwife toads and painted frogs, the males and females generally look much alike. In some species, such as the Iberian and Mallorcan midwife toads, the male is a bit smaller but otherwise looks very much like the female.

The family as it is listed here includes only the midwife toads and painted frogs. Some people, however, add fire-bellied toads and barbourulas to this family. This book lists them under their own family, called Bombinatoridae.

GEOGRAPHIC RANGE

These frogs are mainly European, living in both central and southern Europe. Some also live in northwestern Africa and Israel.

HABITAT

Besides looking different, midwife toads and painted frogs spend their time in different habitats. The painted frogs stay nearer—and often in—the water and are particularly fond of rocky-bottomed, swift-flowing streams, although some live very well in small ponds that may dry up during part of the year. Many will only go into freshwater areas, but some, such as the Tyrrhenian painted frogs, survive in somewhat salty water. When the painted frogs hop onto land, they stay along the shoreline or in areas where the ground is at least somewhat moist. The midwife toads prefer drier areas, like forests and meadows, but they never stray too far from a stream or pond. Both the midwife toads and the painted frogs stay out of sight during the day by crawling under rocks and logs or hiding in burrows that they dig.

DIET

Their diets may include beetles, caterpillars, grasshoppers, flies, and other insects, as well as other types of invertebrates (in-VER-teh-brehts), which are animals without backbones. These invertebrates may include spiders, pillbugs, and snails. Although their tongues do not flick out of their mouths, as do the long tongues of many other species of frogs, they have no trouble snapping up prey right into their mouths.

BEHAVIOR AND REPRODUCTION

Midwife toads and painted frogs are mainly active at night, which is when they hunt for food. During the day, they remain hidden under logs and rocks or in burrows. Not all of the members of this family dig their own burrows, but those that do, like the species that is known simply as a painted frog, use their front legs and toes to scrape their way into sandy ground head-first. They may pat firm the top of the burrow as they dig by butting the head up against it. Sometimes the frog digs only shallow burrows that go little farther than the length of its body, but at other times, the frog may dig a deeper, longer system with side tunnels. When the frogs leave their hiding spots at night, they tend to stay in fairly moist areas to look for food.

The males of all species call during the breeding season either from the water or from shoreline spots on land. In some species, the call sounds like chiming bells, and in others it sounds more like a series of high-pitched "poo" or "pie" noises. Unlike most other species of frogs, some females in this family also call. The Iberian midwife toad, for example, calls back when the male calls. Her call is similar, but quieter than his. Studies of the Iberian midwife toads show that females respond better to males who make faster but lower-pitched calls. Both male and female Mallorcan midwife toads also call. Some scientists believe that their calls do more than bring males and females together to mate. Their studies suggest that the toads, especially the youngest froglets—those that have just made the change from tadpoles—may listen to the calls simply to find out where other toads are, so they can join them in a safe place.

When a male and female mate, the male climbs onto her back and hangs on just above her back legs. From this position, she releases her eggs, and he releases sperm, which unite to start development. Here again, the painted frogs do things differently from the midwife toads. The female painted frogs may mate many times a night, laying up to 1,000 eggs in a single 24-hour period, and she may have more than one mating day in a year. The Iberian painted frog, for example, may mate on six separate days a year and lay a total of 1,500 eggs in a year. Females drop their eggs into the water, where they either stay on the surface or sink to the bottom. The eggs hatch into tadpoles several days later. The exact timing of the hatch depends on the temperature of the water. In Iberian midwife toads, for example, eggs in warm water can hatch in just two days, but eggs in cold water may need six days before they are ready to hatch. The young then remain in the tadpole stage until the next spring or summer, when they change into froglets. When they reach 3 to 5 years old, the young are adults and old enough to mate themselves.

The midwife toads are very unusual in the way their eggs develop. The process starts when the female lays strings of eggs, one string at a time. After 10 minutes or so, the male collects the strings and wraps them around his ankles, one after the other. By the time he is done twirling them around his legs, the male is wearing what looks like a skirt of beads. A single male may mate with several females, and some, like the Iberian midwife toad, may carry up to 180 eggs from four different females. The eggs of the Mallorcan midwife toad are larger, but fewer in number. The Iberian midwife toad's eggs are about one-tenth of an inch (2.6 to 3.5 millimeters) in diameter, and the female may lay 40 to 50 eggs at a time. The female Mallorcan midwife toad typically lays only a dozen or fewer eggs, but her eggs are twice the size at about two-tenths of an inch (5.4 to 7 millimeters) in diameter.

Regardless of the size or number of eggs, the male continues to wear and protect them until they are ready to hatch. At that time, he hops over to the water to allow the newly hatched tadpoles to swim off on their own. This unusual behavior of the male gives the toads their name: midwife toads. A midwife is a person who helps a woman deliver her baby. Although the

HUMAN-CAUSED EXTINCTION

One of the Earth's frogs disappeared in the 1950s at the hands of humans. At that time, people in Israel were trying to fight a dangerous, fever-causing disease called malaria (muh-LAIR-ee-uh). The disease spreads through the bites of infected mosquitoes. One of the people's answers was to drain the swamps where the mosquitoes lived. Without water, the mosquitoes would die out, and the disease would vanish, too. The water disappeared, but the mosquitoes were not the only animals affected. The swamps were also home to other animals, including the Hula painted frog. Unlike the mosquitoes, which exist in Israel to this day, the Hula painted frog could not survive the destruction of its home and is now extinct.

male toad doesn't help the female bear her eggs, he does help make sure they hatch. Tadpoles of the midwife toads can grow quite quickly. Those of the Mallorcan midwife toad, for instance, can double their size and double it again in just a few weeks. Tadpoles make the change to toadlets, a process called metamorphosis (MEH-tuh-MORE-feh-sis), early the following spring and generally are old enough to mate when they reach their second year.

MIDWIFE TOADS, PAINTED FROGS, AND PEOPLE

People rarely see these toads and frogs in the wild. Scientists, however, are especially interested in the midwife toads for the unusual way the males care for the eggs. In most frogs, neither the male nor the female play any part in guarding the eggs or rearing the young.

CONSERVATION STATUS

Of the 10 species in this family, the World Conservation Union (IUCN) considers one as already Extinct, or no longer living, and three others as Vulnerable, which means that they face a high risk of extinction in the wild. It also ranks two others as Near Threatened, which means that they are likely to qualify for a threatened category in the near future.

The Extinct species is the Hula painted frog, which once lived in Israel and possibly Syria. Scientists know about this species from just five specimens, the last of which was collected in 1955. Since then, no other specimens have been found. It probably disappeared as a result of damage to its habitat, especially when people drained the wetlands where it lived in an attempt to wipe out mosquitoes and to turn the swamp into farmland.

The Vulnerable species are the Betic midwife toad and the Mallorcan midwife toad of Spain and the Corsican midwife toad of France. Habitat loss and destruction have hurt the Betic and Corsican toads, while the Mallorcan midwife toad faces threats from new species that have come into its habitat. These new animals, known as introduced species, include a snake and a frog. The snake, called a viperine snake, eats both adult Mallorcan midwife toads and their tadpoles. The new frog, known as the Iberian green frog or Iberian water frog, is taking away food and space from the Mallorcan midwife toad and causing the toad's numbers to drop. By the mid-1980s, conservationists had begun taking steps to protect the toad. In one effort, they have captured some toads so they could breed them in captivity and return the newborn toads to some areas where they had once lived but have since disappeared. This has been very successful, and soon three populations of these reintroduced toads had begun breeding in the wild. Conservationists are now trying to create new watering holes so they can raise and release additional toads in places that are free of animals that might eat them or compete with them for available food.

The toads are doing much better since these efforts began. In 1996, the IUCN considered the species to be Critically Endangered, which meant that it faced an extremely high risk of extinction in the wild. Just eight years later, in 2004, the IUCN saw such improvement in the toad's numbers that it took the species off the Critically Endangered list and now considers it to be Vulnerable, which means that it is at a lower risk of becoming extinct. The Mallorcan midwife toad is unusual for another reason. Until the late 1900s, scientists thought that it had become extinct 2,000 years ago, and all they would ever see were its fossils. They were stunned in 1980, when they learned of a living population that had turned up in a remote, mountainous area. Shortly after this discovery, however, the invading viperine snakes and Iberian green frogs were already taking their toll on the toads and lowering their numbers.

Midwife toad (*Alytes obstetricans*)

MIDWIFE TOAD
Alytes obstetricans

Physical characteristics: The midwife toad is a small, plump toad that sits low to the ground. Its tan to gray skin is spotted in black, brown, and greenish colors and is covered with tiny warts. These warts, which often sit in the middle of a dark spot, give the toad a rough look. In addition, a single row of red-tipped warts runs down each side of its back from behind the eardrum and over two larger warts to the hind leg. The two warts, each of which forms almost a ridge behind the eardrum, are called paratoid (pair-RAH-toyd) glands. These glands and the other warts on its back contain poison and help protect the toad from predators, which find that the poison tastes bad. The toad's large head has a rounded snout and big, copper-colored eyes with vertical slits for pupils. Its underside is off-white, often with gray speckles toward the front. The midwife toad has chubby legs and

The male midwife toad wraps long strings of eggs around his hind feet and protects them until they hatch. (Photograph by Nuridsany et Pérennou. Photo Researchers, Inc. Reproduced by permission.)

no webbing between its toes. Unlike many other frogs that have small, somewhat weak front legs, the midwife toad's forelegs are quite strong. The soles of its front feet have bumps, called tubercles (TOO-ber-kulz). It usually grows to 2.2 inches (5.5 centimeters) long from the tip of its snout to the end of its rump. The males are usually a bit smaller than the females.

Geographic range: The midwife toad is a European species, living in a small area in the Netherlands, in all but the coastal region of Belgium, and in much of Portugal and Spain, as well as France, Germany, Luxembourg, and Switzerland.

Habitat: The midwife toad lives in mountain ponds and slow-moving streams that are filled with water all year long and in nearby hiding places on land. Sometimes, they crawl into mostly bare, sandy soils; beneath small stones as well as large slabs of stone; and inside cracks in walls. All of these spots provide a moist, and at least somewhat warm, shelter for the toads.

Diet: The adults eat various invertebrates, including pillbugs, snails, and different insects.

Behavior and reproduction: During the day, these toads remain out of sight under stones, inside the cracks in stone walls, and in other hideaways where they are shielded from the drying wind and temperature swings. They are also able to use their forelegs to dig head-first into loose gravel and make burrows that they use as shelter. They become active as the sun sets and spend their nights looking for things to eat. They spend the winter in their hideaways, but come out in the early spring to begin mating. The mating season for these toads may begin as early as February in some areas, and it continues through the summer. At night, the male performs his mating call, which is a "poo" sound that he makes once every second or so. He may further prepare a female for mating by tickling her with his toes. They mate with the male on her back and clinging to her waist.

About 10 to 15 minutes after the female lays her strings of eggs, the male scoops them up and wraps them around his legs. He carries them there until they hatch. He may mate with more than one female and sometimes carries as many as 150 eggs at a time. As the eggs grow and become bigger, they look like large dark beads. The male stops now and then to soak the eggs in water. This keeps the eggs moist. When they are ready to hatch in about three to six weeks, the male again hops to the water. There, the tadpoles squirm out of the eggs and into the water. The tadpoles wait until the next spring when they are about 2 to 3.1 inches (5 to 8 centimeters) long to change into toadlets. Over the winter, they usually remain in the water. They are mature enough to mate when they are about 2 years old.

Midwife toads and people: Because of their secretive habits, people rarely see these toads in the wild. Scientists still find them to be fascinating creatures and are especially interested in the male's care of the young.

Conservation status: This species is not considered to be at risk. Conservationists are still watching it closely, however, because some populations of this toad have vanished or are losing numbers. The cause may be habitat destruction and possibly the introduction to the streams of fish that prey on the toads.   ■

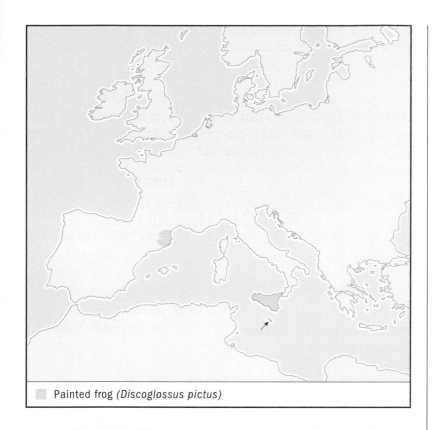

Painted frog (*Discoglossus pictus*)

PAINTED FROG
Discoglossus pictus

Physical characteristics: The painted frog is a rather wide, little frog with long hind limbs and shorter, but stocky forelegs. Its front feet have no webs between the toes, but the back toes are webbed. It is yellowish to greenish brown with long, dark, greenish brown markings. The markings may be bands or oval spots and are sometimes outlined in a lighter color. They usually have a brown band between the eyes. Often, just behind the barely noticeable eardrum, they have a thin paratoid gland that reaches back like a little ridge. The frog has a wide head with a rather pointy snout and big eyes centered with pupils that have shapes described as either hearts or upside down teardrops. Its back has scattered warts. The typical painted frog grows to 2.8 to 3.1 inches (7 to 8 centimeters) long.

Geographic range: Painted frogs live along the Mediterranean Sea in the northeastern African countries of Tunisia, Algeria, and Morocco; in Sicily, which is a southern island of Italy; and on the small Mediterranean islands of Malta and Gozo. Some have also been introduced to areas in France and Spain.

Habitat: Painted frogs live in freshwater and sometimes somewhat salty waters, usually preferring streams or small puddles. People often see them at night in the water filling tire ruts or the hoof prints of cattle. They frequently live near humans, making their homes in orchards or other farm fields, in wells and canals, or in campgrounds.

Diet: Their diet includes insects and other invertebrates.

Behavior and reproduction: Painted frogs use their strong front legs to dig burrows under stones, where they hide during the daytime. At night, they become active and begin looking for food. Their mating season runs almost all year—from January to early November. The males go to the water and give a call that sounds somewhat like the hushed chuckle a person might make in a library. To mate, a male climbs onto the female's back, grabbing her above her hind legs. Over the next half hour to two hours, she lays as many as 50 eggs while the male clings to her back. Afterward and on that same night, she may mate with many other males. The busiest of females may mate with about 20 different males and lay one thousand eggs in a single night. She drops her eggs one by one. They either clump together on the water surface or sink. In about six days, the eggs hatch into tadpoles, which change into froglets one to three months later. The froglets continue to grow and are mature enough to mate the following year.

Painted frogs and people: Because the females can lay so many eggs over a very short time, scientists sometimes use them in laboratory experiments, which may study how eggs develop.

Conservation status: This species is not considered to be at risk. In some places, however, farmlands have disappeared, and the frogs have vanished with them. ■

FOR MORE INFORMATION

Books:

Arnold, E. Nicholas. *Reptiles and Amphibians of Europe (Princeton Field Guides).* Princeton, NJ: Princeton University Press, 2003.

Arnold, E. N., J. A. Burton, and D. W. Ovenden. *Reptiles and Amphibians of Britain & Europe (Collins Field Guide).* London: HarperCollins Publishing Limited, 1999.

Duellman, William E., and Linda Trueb. *Biology of Amphibians.* Baltimore: Johns Hopkins University Press, 1994.

Gasc, Jean-Pierre, et al., eds. *Atlas of Amphibians and Reptiles in Europe.* Paris: Societas Europea Herpetologica and Muséum National d'Histoire, 1997.

Miller, Sara Swan. *Frogs and Toads: The Leggy Leapers.* New York: Franklin Watts, 2000.

Zug, George R., Laurie J. Vitt, and Janalee P. Caldwell. *Herpetology.* 2nd edition. San Diego: Academic Press, 2001.

Web sites:

"Discoglossidae." *AmphibiaWeb.* http://elib.cs.berkeley.edu/aw/lists/Discoglossidae.shtml (accessed on February 7, 2005).

"*Discoglossus nigriventer.*" *Recently Extinct Animals.* http://home.hetnet.nl/harrie.maas/speciesinfo/palestinianpaintedfrog.htm (accessed on February 7, 2005).

"Mallorcan Midwife Toad Saved from Extinction." *Durrell Wildlife Conservation Trust.* http://www.durrellwildlife.org/index.cfm?p=295 (accessed on February 7, 2005).

"The Mallorcan Midwife Toad." *Durrell Wildlife Conservation Trust.* http://www.durrellwildlife.org/index.cfm?p=60 (accessed on February 7, 2005).

family
CHAPTER

PHYSICAL CHARACTERISTICS

With its round and flat body and tiny, pointy-snouted head, the Mesoamerican burrowing toad is an odd-looking creature. It is so unusual, in fact, that some people might not even guess it is a type of frog until they see its hind legs and webbed feet sticking barely out from the saggy skin of its back. The skin droops along the sides of the body and up by the front legs, too. Its legs are short and pudgy, but very strong. The back legs are longer than the front legs, but the front legs are quite thick, as if the frog were a bodybuilder. The edges of the feet also have large, shovel-like bumps that help the frog dig. The toes of its front feet are much shorter than its very long back toes. It typically sits with its hind legs bent up against the body, so they almost disappear. In all, it looks like a dark, round blob with four feet poking out the sides. The head is little more than a cone-shaped lump on the front of the frog. It is small and has no obvious neck supporting it. The reason that the head looks so small is that the frog's shoulders are much closer to the head than they are in other types of frogs. The shoulder blades even wrap around the back of the head, which makes the frog look as if it is always shrugging up its shoulders.

The frog has two dark, small, round, beady eyes, two even smaller nostrils sitting just in front of the eyes on the top of the short snout, and thick lips. Most of the skin on this frog is smooth, but the skin on the snout is tough because it is covered with hard bumps, called spicules (SPIK-yuhlz), that can only be seen with a microscope. The spicules are rounded on the bottom of the snout, but pointy on top. In many other frog species, two eardrums are easily seen on the sides of the head, but the tiny head peeking out from the shoulders in the Mesoamerican burrowing toad leaves no room for any eardrums to show.

Its tongue is different, too. The Mesoamerican burrowing toad does not have a long tongue to flip far out of its mouth as many other frogs do. Instead, it has a sticky, triangular-shaped tongue that it can stick straight out just a little way. Its mouth is toothless.

The frog also has an unusual pattern on its thick back skin that helps to tell it apart from other species. Its back is dark grayish brown, sometimes nearly black, with a single, thin, stripe of yellow, orange, or reddish orange running down the middle. This stripe may be broken here and there, but it is still obvious. It also has yellow and/or orange spots or blotches on either side of the stripe that continue down its sides. Its legs may have a few spots, but the limbs are mostly just grayish brown, and the webbing is typically a lighter gray or bluish color. Its head is also a little lighter in color than the back and may be light gray to light brown. Its underside is dark brown, gray, or bluish gray and has none of the speckles, spots, or stripes of the back.

A HOLE IN ONE

Tadpoles breathe through their gills. Water rushes in; blood in the gills removes the oxygen from the water, and the water flows out through a tiny hole on the tadpole's side. This tiny hole is called a spiracle (SPIH-reh-kul). Tadpoles of the Mesoamerican burrowing toad, clawed frogs, and Surinam toads have two spiracles instead of one, and they are located on the bottom of the tadpole instead. Partly because they have the extra spiracle and because of the location of the two holes, scientists think that these three groups of frogs are very closely related.

The name "toad" in this species can be confusing, because it is not actually a toad at all. The only true toads are in the family Bufonidae. They have warty skin and short legs. The Mesoamerican burrowing toad has smooth skin and quite large hind legs. Even though its common name includes the word "toad," scientists consider it to be a frog and not a true toad. This is a small- to medium-sized frog, and the adults grow to 1.8 to 2.6 inches (4.5 to 6.5 centimeters) long from the tip of the snout to the end of the rump.

The tadpole of the Mesoamerican burrowing toad also looks a bit different from the average tadpole. It has the typical head and long tail, but the head is wider and flatter than other tadpoles, and it has unusual, tiny, fleshy "whiskers" poking from the front of the mouth. These bits of flesh are called barbels

(BAR-bulls). Unlike most other frog species, these tadpoles do not have horny beaks on their mouths. Other tadpoles use these beaks to scrape algae (AL-jee), or tiny plantlike organisms that live in water, off rocks or plants for their meals. The Mexican burrowing toad tadpole eats instead by sifting out little bits of floating algae from the water. The only other tadpoles that look like the burrowing toad tadpoles are those of the Pipidae family, which include the clawed frogs and Surinam toads that live mostly in South America and Africa. Like the Mesoamerican burrowing toad, the clawed frogs and Surinam toads also have a very unusual look that includes an oddly flat head. Scientists believe that these two families of frogs are very closely related because the tadpoles are so much alike and because of some details in their skeletons. Paleontologists (PAY-li-un-TA-luh-jists), or scientists who study fossils, at the Carnegie Museum of Natural History are also now studying a new fossil discovered at Dinosaur National Monument, which is located in Colorado and Utah. This fossil may be a newly discovered relative of the two families.

GEOGRAPHIC RANGE

This family has only one living species, which may be called a Mesoamerican burrowing toad, Mexican burrowing toad, or simply, a burrowing toad. It is found in North and Central America. In North America, it lives in the southernmost part of Texas and in Mexico. It also is found in the Central American countries of Honduras, Guatemala, Belize, El Salvador, Nicaragua, and Costa Rica. At one time, other burrowing toads lived on Earth as far north as Canada. Two now-extinct species lived in what is now Wyoming about 40 to 50 million years ago, and another lived in Saskatchewan, which is in western Canada, about 32 million years ago. Scientists learned about these three species from fossils collected from the two places.

HABITAT

The Mesoamerican burrowing toad mainly lives in underground burrows in lowland areas, which are nearer the Gulf of Mexico and Pacific Ocean and away from the hilly, mountainous regions farther inland. Some live in grassland areas, but others do well in forests that become very dry for part of the year. They can exist in tropical areas or in somewhat cooler subtropical grasslands and forests.

DIET

Although scientists know of no one who has actually seen them eating, they think that the Mesoamerican burrowing toad eats ants and termites that it finds in its underground burrows. They learned this by capturing some of these frogs and looking at what was in their stomachs. This is a somewhat common way for scientists to learn about the diet of animals that live most of their lives out of human sight. Based on the frog's short tongue, scientists believe that this frog digs through the soil until it pops just the tip of its snout into a termite or ant tunnel. From there, it can sit still to wait for one of the insects to crawl by and then quickly stick out its short, gummy tongue to pick up the insects one at a time and gobble them down. This type of sit-and-wait hunting is called ambush (AM-bush) hunting. Tadpoles, which live in pools of water, feed by sucking in water and picking out little bits of algae. This is called filter feeding.

Even though the Mesoamerican burrowing toad's common name includes the word "toad," scientists consider it to be a frog, and not a true toad. (© Tom McHugh/Steinhart Aquarium/Photo Researchers, Inc.)

BEHAVIOR AND REPRODUCTION

The frog uses its strong legs to dig backwards into the ground. As its legs work, the frog twists while blowing up its body with air and then letting the air out. When it is deep enough into the soil, the dirt falls in on top of the frog and eventually covers up the tunneling frog completely. It stays underground most of the time, coming up to the surface during the rainy season, which is when it mates. It may leave its burrows and move above ground at night to look for food, but its large body and short legs make it rather clumsy on land.

The breeding season begins when the heavy rains come. Sometimes, the males make a few calls from their burrows, but they do most of their calling once they find little pools of water. These can be puddles in a farm field, water-filled ditches along a road, or any other small watering hole that forms when the rains come. Males do not breed in ponds that have water in them all year long. From its pool of water, the male begins calling. In many species of frogs, one or two vocal sacs inflate when they call, and each sac looks like a balloon that blows up around its chin. The burrowing toad's sac stays on the inside of its body, so when it fills up with air, the frog's entire body blows up.

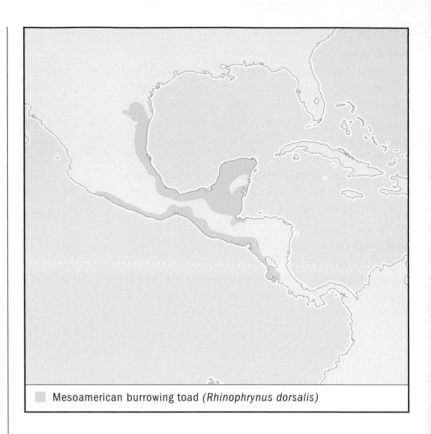

Mesoamerican burrowing toad *(Rhinophrynus dorsalis)*

Every time the male makes his loud mooing call, the air rushes out of his body and pushes the frog backward in the water. Since the male may make its short "ooo" calls 15 to 20 times a minute, the frog continues to scoot around the water backward.

A female comes to a breeding pool, which may contain many males, and picks out a mate by bumping her snout into his chest and throat. He responds by climbing onto her back and grabs onto her with his forelegs just in front of her back legs. She lays a few eggs at a time, sometimes only one, and may mate with different males on several different days, especially if the area gets more than one drenching rain. By the end of the breeding season, each female may have produced thousands of eggs. After she lays the eggs, they sink to the bottom of the water, where they hatch into tadpoles a few days later. The tadpoles group closely together, forming living balls of tadpoles. The larger tadpole balls can reach 3.3 feet (1 meter) in diameter. The tadpoles change into froglets in one to three months. If the water is warmer, they make the change, called metamorphosis (MEH-tuh-MORE-feh-sis), sooner. In cooler water, metamorphosis occurs later.

MESOAMERICAN BURROWING TOADS AND PEOPLE

If enough frogs are calling at once, the noise sounds something like running machinery, and people sometimes hear this so-called chorus (KOR-us) of breeding calls from up to a mile away. Outside of the breeding season, however, people rarely see this frog. It is not popular in the pet trade. It did, however, draw at least a little attention in 2004 when a part-time stuntman rode his unicycle in Death Valley, California, to raise awareness of the Mesoamerican burrowing toad.

CONSERVATION STATUS

This species is not considered to be at risk. It is quite common in parts of Mexico and Central America, but it is rare in the United States and only lives in a few scattered areas in Texas. For this reason, Texas Parks and Wildlife lists it as threatened.

FOR MORE INFORMATION

Books:

Lee, Julian C. *The Amphibians and Reptiles of the Yucatán Peninsula.* Ithaca, NY: Comstock Publishing Associates, Cornell University Press, 1996.

Meyer, John R., and Carol F. Foster. *A Guide to the Frogs and Toads of Belize.* Malabar, FL: Krieger, 1996.

Web sites:

Beaudry, B. 1999. *"Rhinophrynus dorsalis." Animal Diversity Web.* http://animaldiversity.ummz.umich.edu/site/accounts/information/Rhinophrynus_dorsalis.html (accessed on February 10, 2005).

Cannatella, David. "Rhinophrynidae." *Texas Memorial Museum, University of Texas.* http://www.zo.utexas.edu/research/salientia/rhinophrynidae/rhinophrynidae.html (accessed on February 10, 2005).

"Family Rhinophrynidae (Burrowing Toad)." *Animal Diversity Web.* http://animaldiversity.ummz.umich.edu/site/accounts/information/Rhinophrynus_dorsalis.html (accessed on February 10, 2005).

"Mexican Burrowing Toad." *Amphibian Conservation Alliance.* http://www.frogs.org/amphibianet/species.asp?Genus=Rhinophrynus&Species=dorsalis (accessed on February 10, 2005).

"Mexican Burrowing Toad." *eNature, National Wildlife Federation.* http://www.enature.com/fieldguide/showSpeciesFT.asp?fotogID=1098&curPageNum=4&recnum=AR0712 (accessed on February 10, 2005).

family

CHAPTER

PHYSICAL CHARACTERISTICS

With their flat bodies and their wide and fishlike heads, the clawed frogs and Surinam toads are an odd-looking bunch. The head is flat in some species and shaped like a wedge—taller in the back and tapering down toward the front—in others. They have tiny eyes on the top of the head, but they do not have tongues. Their eardrums do not show on the sides of their heads, as they do in many other frogs. Another unusual feature is the line of stitchlike marks that run down each side of the body from the head to the rump. The marks are not actually stitches but allow the frog to feel the movements made by other animals in the water. This line of marks is known as a lateral (LAT-eh-rul) line system. While such a system is common in tadpoles and in fishes, it is unusual in adult frogs. The lateral line, which senses vibrations in the water, is helpful in finding prey.

Clawed frogs and Surinam toads have long hind legs with large, fully webbed feet. The webbing may match their foot color, or it may be a different color, such as the orange-yellow of the Müller's plantanna. The forelegs of clawed frogs and Surinam toads are much smaller than their hind limbs, and the thin toes on the front feet in most species do not have any webbing between them. The only members of this family with front toe webbing are the dwarf clawed frogs, which fall into the groups known as *Hymenochirus* and *Pseudhymenochirus*. All except two species, including the Surinam toad, have three claws on each foot. The claws are the second, third, and fourth toes. The outside two toes on each hind foot are clawless. A typical species in this family has a tan, greenish brown, or gray back, usually with dark spots or markings, and a lighter colored underside with dark markings. Depending on the species, they may either have bumpy or smooth skin. The adults of some species grow to 0.8 to 1.2 inches (2 to 3 centimeters) long from the tip of the snout to the end of the rump, but others can reach as much as 4.1 to 6.7 inches (10.4 to 17 centimeters) in length.

None of the 30 species in this family has vocal sacs. In most other species of frogs, the vocal sac looks like one or two bubbles located below the chin that blow up with air and deflate when the frog makes its call. The clawed frogs and Surinam toads do not even have vocal cords, which are the structures inside the throat that most animals, including humans and other mammals, use to make noises. Instead, these frogs have two disks in their throats that move back and forth to produce clicking sounds. Since these frogs do their clicking underwater, the sound travels through the water as a vibration, rather like an underwater ripple. Another frog can hear the clicks through a different disk that sits under its skin and on the side of its head. This disk picks up the vibration and passes it along to the inner ear, which is the part of the ear located inside the head, and the frog hears the click.

FROGS IN SPACE

Four female frogs soared into orbit in 1992 on board the Space Shuttle Endeavor. Their trip was part of an experiment to see whether their eggs could live and grow normally in a gravity-free environment. Scientists treated the females with a chemical that triggered them to lay their eggs. They then added a male frog's sperm to the eggs to begin development. Through experiments like this one, they hope to learn how difficult it may be for humans to live and reproduce in space.

GEOGRAPHIC RANGE

Clawed frogs and Surinam toads live in tropical parts of South America, but not in mountains, and in the central and southern region of Africa, which is known as sub-Saharan Africa. Humans have brought them to other places, including the United States, the United Kingdom, and other parts of Europe and South America.

HABITAT

Members of this family live in many different watering holes including mucky swamps, small pools of water that dry up during part of the year, large ponds that are filled all year long, and slow-flowing rivers and streams. They rarely leave the water. If their pool dries up, they typically burrow into the still-wet muck at the bottom and wait for the rains to return.

DIET

Many of the tadpoles are filter feeders, which means that they suck in water and strain out bits of food that were floating in it. The tadpoles of the dwarf clawed frogs actively hunt down and eat insects and other invertebrates (in-VER-teh-brehts) or animals without backbones that they find in the water. Adult clawed frogs and Surinam toads eat insects, fishes, occasionally their own tadpoles, as well as mammals and birds that may fall into the water. Since they have no tongues, they must lunge at prey and grab it with their mouths. Some use their front feet to stuff their catch farther into their mouths and/or use the claws of their hind limbs to shred their catch before swallowing it down.

BEHAVIOR AND REPRODUCTION

Clawed frogs and Surinam toads spend much of their time floating in the water with their legs held out from the sides of their bodies. Their dark colors blend in with the water, which makes them difficult for predators to see. They are also quite skittish. The common plantanna, for example, will dive to the bottom of its watering hole as soon as it feels the least bit threatened. Clawed frogs and Surinam toads almost always stay in the water, but sometimes, on very rainy nights, these frogs may leave the water and move short distances from one pond to the next. If they happen to live in a pool of water that dries up during part of the year, clawed frogs and Surinam toads typically bury themselves in the muddy bottom and wait for drenching rain to wet the ground again. This underground waiting period is called estivation (es-tih-VAY-shun). During this time, they do not eat and instead live off fat and other stored energy in their bodies. They may estivate for several months at a time.

Although scientists have not studied these water-loving species very closely, they believe the frogs may mate at any time of year, as long as a heavy rain has soaked the land. Both males and females have the throat disks that allow them to make underwater clicking noises. Each species can make three to six different types of clicks, at least one of which is used to signal that mating time has started. Males climb onto the backs of the females to mate. If a male accidentally climbs onto the back of another male, the second male will click differently to tell the other to get off. As the males and females mate, the females of most species drop their eggs in the water. The eggs hatch into tadpoles, some of which have tiny bits of flesh dangling from the edge of the mouth. These fleshy bits, called barbels (BAR-bulls), are feelers.

Female Surinam toads lay and raise their eggs in a more bizarre way. She flips over while she is laying her eggs, and the eggs settle onto her back, where they stick. Her flesh then swells up around the eggs, turning her back into a sponge-like cradle for them. Depending on the species, the eggs may hatch into tadpoles, or they may skip the swimming tadpole stage and hatch right into froglets. Scientists know this type of back cradle occurs in all but one of the Surinam toads. This is the Myers' Surinam toad, and scientists still are not sure how and where its eggs hatch.

CLAWED FROGS, SURINAM TOADS, AND PEOPLE

People rarely see these frogs in the wild, but they are still very important creatures. Scientists have discovered some unusual chemicals in their skin that may be useful in treating illnesses or in preventing infections. One of these substances, first found in the skin of the common plantanna, is called magainin. Magainin is a piece of protein known as a peptide that fights both germs and fungi. Scientists have started to test this peptide and other compounds like it for use on such things as bandages to help cuts and other wounds heal faster. In addition, scientists use these frogs in the laboratory to study the development of their eggs. Common plantannas carry their see-through eggs on their backs, which provides a good view of the young as they grow and develop inside the egg.

CONSERVATION STATUS

Of the 30 species in this family, the World Conservation Union (IUCN) considers one to be Critically Endangered, which means that it faces an extremely high risk of extinction in the wild; two to be Endangered and facing a very high risk of extinction in the wild; and one to be Near Threatened, which places it at risk of becoming threatened with extinction in the future. It also views seven other species as Data Deficient, a category that means the IUCN does not have enough information to make a judgment about their threat of extinction.

The Critically Endangered species is the Lake Oku clawed frog, which lives in a single lake in western Cameroon. The lake currently has no fish in it to prey on the frogs, but conservationists fear that an introduced fish might find its way into the lake and possibly wipe out the entire frog species. The two Endangered species are the Myers' Surinam toad and Gill's plantanna (also known as the Cape clawed toad or Cape plantanna). Myers' Surinam toad lives in a small area in Panama, and Gill's plantanna lives in a tiny part of southwestern South Africa. Habitat loss is a threat to both species. In addition, water pollution appears to be hurting the Myers' Surinam toad.

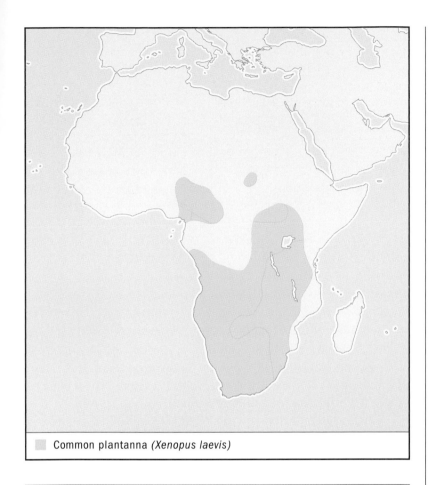

Common plantanna (*Xenopus laevis*)

COMMON PLANTANNA (AFRICAN CLAWED FROG)
Xenopus laevis

Physical characteristics: The common plantanna goes by several different common names, including African clawed frog and clawed toad. It has a flat head and body with long and strong hind legs. Its back and the top of its head are dark-colored, usually gray to olive-brown and sometimes are marked with dark, occasionally orangish, spots. Its underside is lighter colored and may be off-white, light gray, or grayish yellow, sometimes with faint, gray speckles. A thin row of what look like stitches run down each side of the otherwise smooth back from behind the eye to the rump. Each row holds 23 to 31 "stitches." The plantanna has two tiny eyes on top of its wide head and a tiny bit of flesh, called a tentacle, under each eye. It has no

tongue. True to its name, it has little black claws on three toes of each hind foot. The feet are quite large and have gray webbing between and to the tips of the long toes. Sometimes the webbing has a little yellow or orange color to it.

Males and females of this slippery-bodied frog look nearly alike, except that males are smaller. A male grows to about 1.8 to 3.8 inches (4.6 to 9.7 centimeters) long from the tip of the snout to the end of the rump, while females can reach 2.2 to 5.8 inches (5.6 to 14.7 centimeters) long.

Geographic range: The common plantanna is an African frog that lives as far south as South Africa and north to Kenya, Uganda, the Democratic Republic of Congo, and Cameroon. In addition, people have introduced them to many other nations, including England, Germany, Chile, and the United States.

Habitat: The common plantanna is a water-loving species. It can live in all types of water from fast-moving rivers to calm ponds. It can even survive in mucky pools and swamps and in somewhat salty water. Although its native African habitats do not cool much in the winter, it has held up well in places that have winters cold enough to freeze the tops of ponds.

Diet: Tadpoles eat by straining little pieces of algae (AL-jee) and other tidbits from the water. Algae are tiny plantlike organisms that live in water but have no true roots, stems, or leaves. Once the tadpoles change into froglets, their diet switches to insects and other invertebrates they find in the water. Adults also eat young, or larval

(LAR-vuhl), mosquitoes and other insects, sometimes leaping out of the water to nab a flying insect, and will eat larger things, such as fish or birds and mammals that fall into the water. Sometimes they even eat their own eggs and tadpoles.

Behavior and reproduction: Common plantannas stay in the water for almost their entire lives, only coming onto land now and then at night. People most often see them floating at the water's surface, with legs outstretched, and only the top of their heads out of the water. If their pond or swamp dries up, they will dig down into the mud, hind end first, and bury themselves until the rains return.

In addition to signaling the end of estivation for some frogs, the rains combine with warm weather to trigger the mating season for the entire species. Unlike most other types of frogs, both the males and the females call. Their call, which they make underwater, sounds like a buzzing tap. The females lay about one thousand tiny tan eggs, which stick to underwater plants and rocks.

Common plantannas and people: Though it seems strange now, until the 1940s, people turned to these frogs to learn whether a woman was pregnant. To do it, they used a hypodermic needle to suck up a little of the woman's urine and then inject it under the skin of the female frog. If the woman was pregnant, the hormones in her urine would spark the frog to start laying eggs. If the woman was not pregnant, the frogs laid no eggs. Medical professionals now find out if a woman is pregnant through other tests that do not involve frogs.

Nowadays, this species has another role in medicine. One chemical in its skin kills bacteria and may be a useful antibiotic, while another may be helpful in explaining how the human brain works. Besides its importance in medicine, people buy and sell the common plantanna as a pet. Some local people in Africa also once collected the frogs for food.

Conservation status: Because these frogs live in many areas and do well in a variety of different habitats, the species is not considered to be at risk. ■

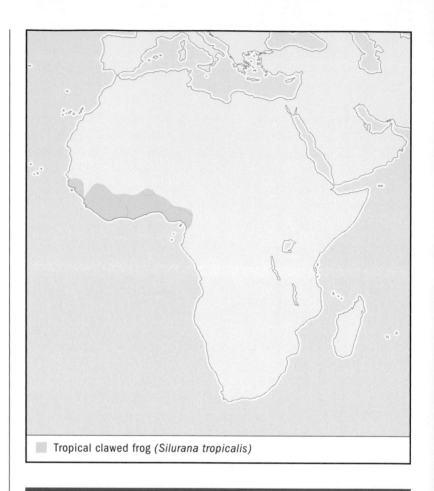

Tropical clawed frog (*Silurana tropicalis*)

TROPICAL CLAWED FROG
Silurana tropicalis

Physical characteristics: If a frog were made of milk chocolate and started to melt, it would look something like the tropical clawed frog. This frog has a light chocolate brown or slightly greenish brown, flat, round blob of a body. Tiny gray and black marks fleck its back, and a row of 18 to 20 "stitches" runs down each side of the body from the eye to the rump. Its underside is white or light gray with some black blotches. It has a small, flat, round head with two beady eyes on top, and a tiny tentacle hanging below each eye. Its hind legs are large and pudgy. When the frog is sitting, its back legs and its much smaller forelegs stick out from the side of the animal, rather than tucking against the body as is common in most other frog species. Three claws

If a frog were made of milk chocolate and started to melt, it would look something like the tropical clawed frog. (Illustration by Michelle Meneghini. Reproduced by permission.)

are visible on its feet. The females are slightly larger than the males and usually grow to 1.7 inches (4.3 centimeters) long from snout to rump. The males typically reach 1.4 inches (3.6 centimeters) long.

Geographic range: Tropical clawed frogs live in western Africa.

Habitat: The tropical clawed frog lives mainly in water within tropical forests, but sometimes it lives in the ponds of grassland areas that are alongside forests. It does not exist in mountain areas.

Diet: From what little is known about its diet, scientists believe the tropical clawed frog eats almost anything it can find, including various invertebrates and tadpoles. They are not sure if it eats its own tadpoles or those of other frogs.

Behavior and reproduction: This frog stays in the water most of the time, but it will move about on land from pond to pond on very rainy nights. They behave differently during the dry season, when water can be scarce. Those that live near rivers hide in holes or under stone and roots during the daytime and sit at night in small, rocky pools of water left standing along the river. Those that live in ponds that lose much of their water in the dry season will bury themselves in the muddy pond bottom.

The tropical clawed frog takes advantage of the year-round warmth of the climate where it lives and may mate whenever a heavy rain drenches the land. The males will make their rattling call at night from large forest ponds or small forest pools. When a male finds a female, he climbs onto her back and holds on above her hind legs to mate with her. She lays her eggs in the water, and the eggs stick to underwater plants.

Tropical clawed frogs and people: People rarely see this frog in the wild, and it is not popular in the pet trade.

Conservation status: This species is not considered to be at risk.   ■

Surinam toad (*Pipa pipa*)

SURINAM TOAD
Pipa pipa

Physical characteristics: The Surinam toad is nothing less than bizarre. Its body is so flat that it appears as if it has been run over. It has a triangular-shaped head that comes to a point at the end of the snout. Its fairly short hind legs have huge, webbed feet. Each of the toes on its short front legs is split at the end into four pieces that almost look like four more small toes, and each of these small "toes" is split again at the tip into two more. It also has tiny, spiny bits of skin poking out from the sides of its mouth. Two tiny eyes may peer out from the top of the head, but sometimes they are completely hidden

The female Surinam toad incubates eggs on her back, which remain there for three or four months. At that time, the eggs hatch right into froglets. (Photograph by Tom McHugh/Steinhart Aquarium. Photo Researchers, Inc. Reproduced by permission.)

underneath flesh. The Surinam toad also has two slits for nostrils on the top of its head. Its body is dark brown, grayish brown, or tan and often has a blotched pattern. Its underside has a T-shaped marking with the top of the T running across the chest. Females are usually a bit larger and can grow to 4 to 7 inches (10.5 to 17.1 centimeters) long from the snout to the rump. The males usually reach no more than 6 inches (15.4 centimeters) long.

Geographic range: The Surinam toad lives in the northern and central parts of South America, including Colombia, Venezuela, Guyana, French Guiana, and Surinam (also sometimes spelled Suriname) in the north, and south into Brazil, Ecuador, Peru, and Bolivia. It also lives on the West Indies island of Trinidad.

Habitat: The Surinam toad lives on the bottoms of mucky ponds and swamps, as well as in slow-flowing streams and rivers through-out the lowland rainforests. It does not live in the mountains.

Diet: This toothless, tongueless frog catches small fish and inverte-brates underwater by lunging at the prey while opening wide its mouth and blowing up its body. This sucks in the water and the prey together. Using its front feet, it pushes the prey farther into its mouth.

Behavior and reproduction: This frog stays still and rests in the mucky water bottom much of the time, but it will move on land from pond to pond on very rainy nights. Because it usually stays out of sight, scientists know little else about its non-mating behavior. Dur-ing the mating season, they call with a sharp clicking noise. The males grab onto the females in piggyback fashion, hanging on in front of her hind legs. The frog pair rolls over while floating in the water, and the female lays three to five eggs while she is in the upside down po-sition. The eggs catch on the male's belly, then drop onto the female's back as the pair completes the roll. Instead of the eggs sticking to vegetation or floating off into the water as they do with most frogs, the eggs stay on the mother's back, where they become caught. Her skin swells up around the sides of each egg. In all, she may have about 50 eggs on her back, which remain there for the next three or four months. At that time, the eggs hatch right into froglets, which pop right out of her back.

Surinam toads and people: Some people eat these frogs.

Conservation status: This species is not considered to be at risk.   ■

FOR MORE INFORMATION

Books:

Channing, Alan. *Amphibians of Central and Southern Africa.* Ithaca, NY: Comstock Publishing Associates, Cornell University Press, 2001.

Halliday, Tim, and Kraig Adler, eds. *The Encyclopedia of Reptiles and Amphibians (Smithsonian Handbooks).* New York: Facts on File, 1991.

Maruska, Edward J. *Amphibians: Creatures of the Land and Water.* New York: Franklin Watts, 1994.

Miller, Sara Swan. *Frogs and Toads: The Leggy Leapers.* New York: Franklin Watts, 2000.

Rödel, Mark-Oliver. *Herpetofauna of West Africa.* Vol. 1, *Amphibians of the West African Savanna.* Frankfurt: Edition Chimaira, 2000.

Tinsley, R. C., and H. R. Kobel, eds. *The Biology of Xenopus.* London: Clarendon Press, 1996.

Web sites:

"African Clawed Frog." *Smithsonian National Zoological Park.* http://nationalzoo.si.edu/Animals/ReptilesAmphibians/Facts/FactSheets/Africanclawedfrog.cfm (accessed on February 14, 2005).

"Frog Facts: About the African Clawed Frog." *Fluffy's Frog Pond.* http://fluffyfrog.com/FrogPondFactsF.html (accessed on February 14, 2005).

"Froggiecam." *Ferrell Lab, Stanford University.* http://www.stanford.edu/group/ferrelllab/frogtank.html (accessed on February 12, 2005).

"Frogs: A Chorus of Colors." *American Museum of Natural History.* http://www.amnh.org/exhibitions/frogs/featured/laboratory.php (accessed on February 14, 2005).

"*Xenopus laevis* African Clawed Frog." *Western Ecological Research Center, San Diego Field Station, U.S. Geological Survey.* http://www.werc.usgs.gov/fieldguide/xela.htm (accessed on February 12, 2005).

ASIAN TOADFROGS
Megophryidae

Class: Amphibia
Order: Anura
Family: Megophryidae
Number of species: 107 species

PHYSICAL CHARACTERISTICS

Most of the Asian toadfrogs have vertical, cat-like pupils, paddle-shaped tongues, and colors and patterns on their heads and backs that blend in with their environment. Some species have warty skin, but others have smooth skin. A few do not have the cat-eye pupils. These include species like the Asian mountain toad, which has a diamond-shaped pupil. The males and females look quite similar for most of the year. In the breeding season, the males of some species develop bright red-, yellow-, or orange-colored spots on their sides and upper legs or some colorful tints on their front toes or on their vocal sacs. The vocal sac is a balloon-like area under the chin that blows up and deflates when the male performs its call. Also during the mating season, the males of some species, including those known as alpine toads and cat-eyed frogs, develop rough patches on the chest and front toes. Male moustache toads are unusual in that they grow spiny "moustaches" when they are ready to mate.

Asian toadfrogs are split into two main groups. One group includes the leaf litter and dwarf litter frogs, the slender mud frogs, the lazy toads, and the moustache toads. All of these frogs have a bump that runs from the second toe onto the first, or big, toe. They usually have large or small "horns" on their eyebrow ridges. The horns are actually pieces of flesh that are pointed. In fact, the name of the family, Megophryidae, is from two Greek words that mean "large eyebrow." Some, like the Asian horned frog, have large, pointed eyebrows. The "horns" on other species are much smaller, and some do not have them

phylum

class

subclass

order

monotypic order

suborder

▲ **family**

at all. This group of frogs has tadpoles with mouths that are pointed upward on their heads and look like funnels. The tadpoles also have a small, fingernail-like beak on the lower jaw.

The other main group of Asian toadfrogs include a variety of mostly large-eyed frogs that have a large bump at the bottom of the second front toe but not on the first toe. Species in this family are the horned frogs, broad-headed frogs, Asian mountain toads, Burmese spadefoot toads, and others. Their tadpoles have larger beaks on both the upper and lower jaws, and mouths that open on the bottom of the head.

The species in this family come in many sizes, too. The smallest only grow to 0.7 inches (1.8 centimeters) long from snout to rump, but the largest top 5.5 inches (14 centimeters) in length. The broad-headed toads can grow to 6.6 inches (16.8 centimeters) long. The females usually outgrow the males, but in the moustache toads, the males are slightly longer.

GEOGRAPHIC RANGE

Asian toadfrogs live in many areas of Southeast Asia and Indonesia.

HABITAT

Although Asian toadfrogs live in many different habitats, most tend to prefer old, thick forests that have ground covered by layers of leaves. Most of them move into clean and clear streams, usually those with slow currents, to breed.

DIET

Many Asian toadfrogs eat a wide variety of invertebrates (in-VER-teh-brehts), or animals without backbones. Some, like the Annam broad-headed toad, are opportunistic (ah-por-toon-ISS-tik) feeders. An opportunistic feeder is an animal that will eat almost anything it can catch, get into its mouth, and swallow. Many Asian toadfrogs hunt by sitting still and waiting for prey to wander by. This type of hunting is called ambush hunting.

BEHAVIOR AND REPRODUCTION

The typical Asian toadfrog spends its days resting under rocks, logs, or leaf piles on land and comes out at night to look for food. They are mostly slow-moving frogs that rarely climb and are not particularly good hoppers or swimmers. The leaf litter frogs, for instance, do a slow, waddling walk on land. A few species, like the Asian mountain toad, do some climbing, especially during the mating season. They climb onto branches above the stream, where they mate. Despite the slow speed of most Asian toadfrogs, they are able to avoid the mouths of predators by blending into the background. Most of them have backs and heads in grays and browns that are similar in color to the leaf piles scattered on the forest floor. Many of them also have horn-like eyebrows that make the frog look like a dead leaf. At the slightest sound, these frogs hunker down and stay still and wait for the predator to pass by. The broad-headed toads have another defense tactic. If a predator comes too close, these frogs will spread open their big mouths and hold them wide. Sometimes the sight frightens off the attacker.

PUT YOUR HEAD ON MY SHOULDER

Some male frogs use other methods besides calling to convince females to mate with them. One of the Asian toadfrogs is the slender mud frog, also known as the mountain short-legged toad, which is a dark-speckled, orange to tan, somewhat warty frog. When a female comes close to a male, he lays his chin on her shoulder, then moves toward a rock in a shallow mountain stream. If she is interested, she follows him, they mate, and she lays her eggs underwater and beneath the rock.

For those that live in cool or dry areas, the mating season begins when rainy weather arrives. Those whose homes are in places that are mild and wet all year may mate over longer periods. During the mating season, the males usually move to stream shores and begin calling. Although a male may make a few half-hearted calls during the day, it mainly does its calling after sundown. Depending on the species, the male's call may sound like a honk, a loud clank, a low bark, a repeating whistle, or some other noise. During mating a male climbs onto the female's back. The males of some species then grasp her at her front legs, while other males hold on to her above her hind legs. The female lays her eggs so they attach, often in clumps, to the bottom of large rocks along the stream's bank. The adults leave, and the eggs soon hatch into tadpoles. The moustache toads mate a bit differently. In these species, several males may group together at a nesting site and, after mating with females, remain with the eggs until they hatch. Tadpoles of many Asian toadfrogs stay in slower parts of the stream, but a few, like the slender mud frog, prefer faster currents in stony streams. Some tadpoles do not change into frogs until they are two years old. A few species, like the Bana leaf litter frog, appear to lay their eggs on land.

ASIAN TOADFROGS AND PEOPLE

People who live near the larger species sometimes eat them, but for the most part, people rarely see any of the Asian toadfrogs. These frogs, however, may prove to be quite important to humans. Since the tadpoles must have clean streams to live and grow, they are good bioindicator (bie-oh-IN-dih-KAY-tor) species. A bioindicator species is an animal that people can use to tell whether the environment is healthy. For example, if a population of Asian toadfrogs were to disappear suddenly from an area, the change might mean that the water in the streams has become polluted.

CONSERVATION STATUS

Of the 107 species in this family, the World Conservation Union (IUCN) considers three species to be Critically Endangered, which means that they face an extremely high risk of extinction in the wild; 14 to be Endangered and facing a very high risk of extinction in the wild; and 26 to be Vulnerable and facing a high risk of extinction in the wild. In addition, 13 are Near Threatened and at risk of becoming threatened with extinction in the future; and 28 others are Data Deficient, which means that the IUCN has too little information to make a judgment about the threat of extinction.

The three Critically Endangered species are the web-footed dwarf litter frog, the Liangbei toothed toad, and the spotted lazy toad. The web-footed dwarf litter frog has a very small population that lives only in one place: near a small, clear, rocky stream in a forest reserve of Sabah, in Malaysian Borneo. Although the stream is inside a reserve, loggers are removing the surrounding forests. Since this species probably spends much of its life in those vanishing forests, it may soon become extinct. The Liangbei toothed toad also lives in a tiny area and breeds in just one small, mountain stream in southern Sichuan province, China. Scientists believe the entire species has fewer than 100 members. The stream is not in a protected area, and the surrounding forests are disappearing to logging. If its forest habitat disappears from logging or from a fire, this frog could easily become extinct. The last of the three Critically Endangered species is the spotted lazy toad, which is known from just a few individuals that were collected in the 1970s from mountains in China. Although scientists have made numerous searches since then, they have not been able to find any more of these frogs and fear they may already be extinct.

Many of the other Endangered, Vulnerable, and Near Threatened species in this family are in danger because their habitat is disappearing, mainly due to people cutting down forests for lumber or to make way for farming or houses. In some cases, the number of frogs is dropping because fertilizers and pollutants are draining into the streams where the frogs have their young. The tadpoles typically cannot survive in anything but clean, clear water. Changes in the habitat are especially dangerous for those species that live in very small areas. In fact, scientists believe that nearly one of every four Asian toadfrog species lives or breeds in only one place, such as a tiny part of a mountain forest or stream. For them, a few days of tree-cutting or a change to one stretch of a stream can wipe out their entire home.

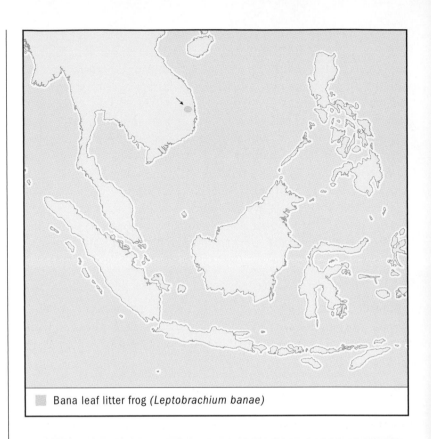

Bana leaf litter frog (*Leptobrachium banae*)

BANA LEAF LITTER FROG
Leptobrachium banae

Physical characteristics: The Bana leaf litter frog has a body that looks too big for its skinny legs. It has a wide head with huge, bulging eyes. The eyes are black on the bottom, white on top, and circled with a thin, white circle. Its back is dark brown with tiny, red spots along the sides and also on its hind legs. Its front and back legs are brown with darker bands continuing down onto its toes. It has a white-spotted gray underside. Adult females can grow to 3.1 to 3.3 inches (8 to 8.4 centimeters) long from the snout to the rump, but adult males typically only reach 2.3 to 2.9 inches (5.7 to 7.3 centimeters) in length.

Geographic range: The Bana leaf litter frog lives in the Gia Lai province of south-central Vietnam and in the Annamite Mountains of Laos.

Habitat: The Bana leaf litter frog lives in thick, evergreen primary forests, which are forests that have never been cut down. These forests are located where the land is higher—between 2,620 and 5,240 feet (800 to 1,600 meters) above sea level.

Diet: The Bana leaf litter frog probably eats insects.

Behavior and reproduction: By day, this frog hides under the leaves that coat the forest ground. It comes out at night to wander about on land. Often, this species actually walks, rather than hops. Unlike many other frogs that mate and lay their eggs in the water, this frog does both on land. People have heard lone males calling from beneath logs and in burrows that are nowhere near a stream. More studies will provide additional information about this species.

Bana leaf litter frogs and people: People rarely see or hear this nighttime frog.

Conservation status: The World Conservation Union (IUCN) considers this species to be Vulnerable, which means that it faces a high risk of extinction in the wild. In Vietnam, its habitat is disappearing as people clear the land for farming or through logging.   ■

Schmidt's lazy toad (*Oreolalax schmidti*)

SCHMIDT'S LAZY TOAD
Oreolalax schmidti

Physical characteristics: Sometimes called the webless toothed toad, the Schmidt's lazy toad is a grayish brown animal with warts dotting its body, thin forelegs, and rather short back legs. All of its legs have dark bands. Their undersides are pinkish tan and almost see-through. Adults grow to 1.7 to 2.0 inches (4.5 to 5.4 centimeters) long from snout to rump. Males are usually just a bit smaller than the females. The males also have many spines on the first toe of each front foot and two, large, rough spots on the chest. These rough spots, called nuptial (NUHP-shul) patches or nuptial pads, help the male hold onto the female's slippery back during mating.

Geographic range: The Hengduanshan Mountains of southern Szechwan and Yunnan, which are located in central to southern China, are home to this species.

Habitat: Schmidt's lazy toad lives in marshes and streams within mountain forests and valleys.

Diet: No one knows what this toad eats.

Behavior and reproduction: Schmidt's lazy toad lives most of its life on land. During mating season, the males begin calling, often from underneath a rock. Unlike most other frogs, they will keep on calling even if a person walks up and flips over their rock, leaving the frog in plain sight. When the males spot a female, they will surround her and continue calling. Male and female pairs mate in the water, and the female lays a sticky ball of about 120 eggs onto the bottom of a stream rock. The eggs hatch into green- and gold-speckled tadpoles, which turn into froglets shortly after breeding season the following year.

Schmidt's lazy toads and people: People and these frogs rarely see one another.

Conservation status: The World Conservation Union (IUCN) considers this species to be Near Threatened, which means that it is at risk of becoming threatened with extinction in the future. Because it lives in a very small area and its numbers are low, any changes to its habitat could be dangerous to this frog. ■

Ailao moustache toad (*Vibrissaphora ailaonica*)

AILAO MOUSTACHE TOAD
Vibrissaphora ailaonica

Physical characteristics: The small spines that stick straight out of the male's upper lip give the Ailao moustache toad, also known as a Yunnan moustache toad, its common name. Its other common name, the Ailao spiny toad, also refers to its prickly lip. The females do not have spines and instead have tiny white spots on the upper lip. They have large eyes that are black on the bottom and bright green on the top and have vertical, cat-like pupils. Their bodies are reddish brown with faint, darker brown spots on the back and pale, dark brown bands on their front legs, unwebbed front toes, back legs, and webbed back toes. Their skin may be very rough and make them look as if they had been dipped in sand. Young frogs are tan instead of reddish brown and have more noticeable spots and bands on their bodies. Unlike many other species in this family, the males are a bit larger than

the females. Males typically reach 3.2 inches (8.2 centimeters) long from snout to rump, while females usually grow to 3.1 inches (7.8 centimeters) in length.

Geographic range: The moustache toad lives in the Ailao Shan and Wuliang Shan mountain ranges in central Yunnan, China, and possibly in northern Vietnam.

Habitat: The moustache toad spends most of the year on land in thick, shady forests high in the mountains, usually between 7,220 to 8,200 feet (2,200 to 2,500 meters) above sea level. During the mating season, it moves into slow-moving, clear streams.

Diet: It appears to eat various invertebrates, such as worms and snails, that it catches on the forest floor.

Behavior and reproduction: The Ailao moustache toad stays on land most of the year, but moves into a stream during the two- to six-week-long mating season in late winter. Several males share a nesting site under a large rock, and each male begins to sprout the 10 to 16 spines in his "moustache." At the same time, the male's front legs become thicker, and the skin on his back and sides starts to droop and become baggy. Females come to the nest, mate with the males, and lay their eggs in the nest. In most other species of frogs, both the male and female leave after the female lays her eggs, and the eggs hatch and develop on their own. In the Ailao moustache toad, however, the females leave, but the males stay with the eggs. The males may continue to mate with other females, who also lay their eggs in the same nest. In about 40 days, the eggs hatch into tadpoles. The brown-colored tadpoles change into froglets in their second year.

Ailao moustache toads and people: Few people have ever seen this frog.

Conservation status: The World Conservation Union (IUCN) considers this species to be Near Threatened, which means that it is at risk of becoming threatened with extinction in the future. The Ailao moustache toad seems to be quite rare. However, most if not all of its habitat is inside nature reserves, where it is protected. ∎

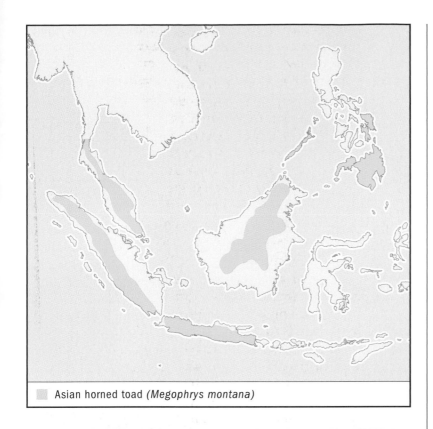

Asian horned toad *(Megophrys montana)*

ASIAN HORNED FROG
Megophrys montana

Physical characteristics: The Asian horned frog, which is sometimes called the Asian spadefoot toad, looks as if it has horns over its dark brown eyes. It is a big-bodied frog with a large head that sometimes has a fleshy lump on the end of its snout. Its back is tan to reddish brown and has several ridges that run from the head to the rump. Its hind legs usually show dark banding, but the bands may be faint. Other than a few small lumps on its back and sides, the frog has smooth skin. Males and females look alike, but the females are usually larger. Females can grow to 2.6 to 4.4 inches (6.7 to 11.1 centimeters) long from snout to rump, while the males usually only reach 1.7 to 3.6 inches (4.4 to 9.2 centimeters) in length.

Geographic range: Asian horned frogs are found in parts of Southeast Asia and Indonesia, including Thailand, Malaysia, the Philippines,

Asian horned toads look for food on the forest floor at night, eating larger invertebrates, such as cockroaches and land snails, as well as scorpions that may be as long as the frogs themselves. (© Suzanne L. Collins & Joseph T. Collins/Photo Researchers, Inc.)

Sumatra, Java, Borneo, and tiny Natuna Island northwest of Borneo.

Habitat: Asian horned frogs live in thick, shady, humid, tropical forests, sometimes high in the mountains. They may also live in farm fields.

Diet: This frog looks for food on the forest floor at night, eating larger invertebrates, such as cockroaches and land snails, as well as scorpions that may be as long as the frog itself.

Behavior and reproduction: This frog takes advantage of its leaf-life body to hide from predators. When it crouches down and sits still, as it does whenever a possibly dangerous animal approaches, the frog looks like any other dead leaf lying on the ground. This ability to stay out of sight is important for this species, because it cannot move very fast on land or in the water, and it does not climb. The Asian horned frog is mainly active at night. During the day, it hides under leaves, logs, or rocks. It stays on land most of the year, but moves to small- and medium-sized streams during the mating season. The male's mating call is a loud, echoing honk or clang. The males appear to call more on nights with a full moon. Females lay their eggs in the water along the shore, and the see-through eggs hatch into brown-colored tadpoles that hide among underwater plants until they change into froglets, which probably happens when they are about two months old.

Asian horned frogs and people: People rarely see this well-camouflaged, nighttime frog in the wild.

Conservation status: This species is not considered threatened or endangered. In the areas where it lives, it is quite common. ■

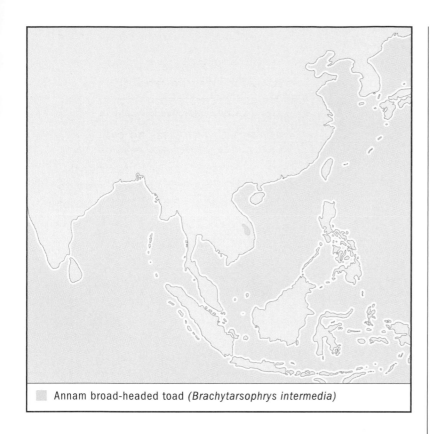

Annam broad-headed toad (*Brachytarsophrys intermedia*)

ANNAM BROAD-HEADED TOAD
Brachytarsophrys intermedia

Physical characteristics: Annam broad-headed toads, also known as Annam spadefoot toads, have so many ridges on their bodies that the head and back almost look as if they are covered with an armor shield. Two ridges begin at the back of the wide head, carry up over the eye to make a pointy eyebrow, then run forward to meet at the tip of the frog's pointed snout. Other, sometimes broken, ridges run from the rear of the head over the broad back or down its sides to the rump. Its head and back are usually light brown to reddish brown. Large for an Asian toadfrog, a female Annam broad-headed toad can grow to 5.5 inches (13.9 centimeters) long from snout to rump. The males are smaller and can reach 4.6 inches (11.8 centimeters) in length.

Geographic range: The Annam broad-headed toads are found in southern central Vietnam.

Annam broad-headed toads, also known as Annam spadefoot toads, have so many ridges on their bodies that the head and back almost look as if they are covered with an armor shield. (Illustration by Bruce Worden. Reproduced by permission.)

Habitat: Annam broad-headed toads live in mountainside forests that are between 2,460 to 3,940 feet (750 to 1,200 meters) above sea level. During mating season, they move into nearby streams.

Diet: This toad is an opportunistic feeder that will eat everything from insects and spiders to small frogs and rodents.

Behavior and reproduction: This frog sits still most of the time and blends into the background, which is useful for ambushing prey and for keeping out of sight of predators. If a predator does spot the frog and approach, the frog will open wide its mouth, which may scare away the predator. Unlike most frogs that mate in the spring, or in the spring and summer, this frog mates early in the spring and also late in the fall. The males move to streams and start calling from a sheltered spot under a large rock. Females come to the streams, mate with the males, and lay their eggs under the rocks.

Annam broad-headed toads and people: People rarely see this frog in the wild.

Conservation status: The World Conservation Union (IUCN) now considers the Annam broad-headed toad to be Vulnerable, which means that it faces a high risk of extinction in the wild. Once a common species, its habitat has disappeared in the past 100 years, and the number of frogs has dropped. ■

FOR MORE INFORMATION

Books:

Cogger, Harold G., and Richard G. Zweifel. *Encyclopedia of Reptiles and Amphibians.* San Diego, CA: Academic Press, 1998.

Inger, Robert F. "Distribution of Amphibians in Southern Asia and Adjacent Islands." In *Patterns of Distribution of Amphibians: A Global Perspective,* edited by William Duellman. Baltimore: Johns Hopkins University Press, 1999.

Zhao, Er-Mi. "Distribution Patterns of Amphibians in Temperate Eastern Asia." In *Patterns of Distribution of Amphibians: A Global Perspective,* edited by William Duellman. Baltimore: Johns Hopkins University Press, 1999.

Web sites:

"Black-eyed Litter Frog." *Ecology Asia.* http://www.ecologyasia.com/verts/amphibians/black-eyed_litter_frog.htm (accessed on February 16, 2005).

"Draft Report Assessing the Impact of Importing Live Asian Horned Frog (*Megophrys montana*) into Australian Zoos." *Australian Government Department of the Environment and Heritage.* http://www.deh.gov.au/biodiversity/trade-use/publicnotices/archive/draft-report/m-montana.html#range (accessed on February 17, 2005).

"Frogs in Kerinci Seblat." *Kerinci Seblat National Park.* http://www.kerinci.org/about_frog.html (accessed on February 17, 2005).

"Malayan Horned Frog." *Ecology Asia.* http://www.ecologyasia.com/verts/amphibians/malayan_horned_frog.htm (accessed on February 16, 2005).

"Mountain Litter Frog." *Ecology Asia.* http://www.ecologyasia.com/verts/amphibians/mountain_litter_frog.htm (accessed on February 16, 2005).

"Spotted Litter Frog." *Ecology Asia.* http://www.ecologyasia.com/verts/amphibians/spotted_litter_frog.htm (accessed on February 16, 2005).

"Yunnan Moustache Toad." *Science Museums of China.* http://www.kepu.com.cn/english/animal/class/cls404.html (accessed on February 16, 2005).

Class: Amphibia

Order: Anura

Family: Pelobatidae

Number of species: 11 species

family

CHAPTER

phylum

class

subclass

order

monotypic order

suborder

▲ family

PHYSICAL CHARACTERISTICS

The spadefoot toads are named for the small scoops, or spades, on the bottoms of their hind feet. They use their spades, which are made of the same material as fingernails, to move away the dirt as they burrow into the soil. The spadefoot toad is actually not a true toad. All true toads are grouped into the family called Bufonidae. Spadefoot toads do look a bit like true toads, because they have round, plump bodies, but they do not have very warty skin. Their skin is actually quite smooth and moist, although tiny lumps are sometimes noticeable on their backs. These small lumps may be tipped in red. In addition, spadefoot toads also have teeth on the upper jaw. True toads do not.

Many of the species in this family have brown to gray backs, sometimes with faint stripes or spots, and light-colored bellies. Their eyes have vertical, catlike pupils. Some, like the Great Basin spadefoot, have a large lump between the eyes. Depending on the species, adults may grow to 2 to 3.2 inches (5.1 to 8.1 centimeters) from the tip of the snout to the end of the rump.

Their eggs are tiny and typically dark brown. The tadpoles are usually tan to brown in color. Some have orange speckles and see-through tails.

GEOGRAPHIC RANGE

Four species live from Europe and western Asia to northwestern Africa. The remaining seven are North American species, found from southern Mexico through the United States and to southern Canada.

HABITAT

Spadefoot toads are burrowing frogs that live in areas with loose, often sandy soil and usually dry weather. Some, like the Plains spadefoot toad, can live in almost desert-like conditions. They come above ground, usually at night following a heavy rain or when the air is humid, to find food. Spring rains also bring the frogs onto land for mating. Those that live in the driest of places, however, may stay underground for all but two weeks of the year.

DIET

Unlike most other frog species, the tadpoles of spadefoot toads are not just vegetarians. They will suck in water and sift out bits of plants, as some other species of tadpoles do, but they will search the water to catch and eat insects and other invertebrates (in-VER-teh-brehts), which are animals without backbones. Once they become frogs, they switch to an all-meat diet and eat snails, spiders, earthworms, and various insects, including beetles, grasshoppers, and caterpillars.

BEHAVIOR AND REPRODUCTION

The spadefoot toads are burrowing frogs that spend their days and many of their nights underground where the ground is moist. They use the spades on their feet to dig rump-first into the ground. They shovel with one foot at a time and wiggle their bodies backwards into the burrow. During the rainy season, their burrows are only a couple of inches (5 centimeters) deep, but during long dry times, they may burrow down 3 feet (1 meter) or more. On rainy nights, or nights that are humid, they will come above ground to look for food. They need the moisture in the air because they can die if their skin dries out. When the soil becomes dry even deep below the surface, these frogs may snuggle inside layers of their own dead skin to keep themselves at least slightly moist and away from the dry soil, which might soak up what little moisture they have. They can survive inside these cocoons of dead skin for many weeks.

Because they stay underground much of the year, the spadefoot toads can avoid many of their predators. Even when they are above ground, the browns and grays of their skin can help to hide them from hungry eyes, especially if they stay perfectly still. If a predator does spot them, the frogs can defend

NO RELATIVE OF MINE

For many years, scientists had thought the Asian toadfrogs and spadefoot toads were so similar that they should both be placed in the same group, called a family. Closer studies revealed that the two were much more different than originally thought, and in 1985 scientists separated the toadfrogs into their own family.

themselves by sucking air into their lungs and blowing up their bodies to make them look bigger than they are. Their larger bodies might be enough to frighten away certain predators. Some species, like the eastern spadefoot toad, have skin that gives off bad-tasting and often smelly ooze that might discourage a predator. Despite all of these defense tactics, these frogs sometimes become lunch for their predators, including birds, such as owls and crows; mammals, like coyotes; and snakes.

Dangers aside, the spadefoot toads leave the protection of their underground burrows to mate on land. The sound of rain drumming on the ground overhead brings out hundreds of male spadefoot toads, which hop to puddles or shallow ponds and begin calling while floating in the water. Depending on the species, the calls may sound like crows cawing, sheep baaing, or a finger squeaking against a balloon. The calls can become quite loud, and people have reported hearing them from a mile (1.6 kilometers) away. In the water pools, the males set up territories and keep their distance from one another. The males call most at night, but may also call sometimes during the day. The females arrive and select mates. To mate, a male climbs onto a female's back and clings to her with his forelegs wrapped just in front of her hind legs. The eggs, which can number several hundred to more than a thousand per female, stream from her body and stick in clumps to underwater plants, stones, and other items. The eggs usually hatch into tadpoles within a week. If the weather is especially warm, they may hatch in just one to three days.

Dry weather is always a threat to a tadpole, which must turn into a froglet before its watering hole evaporates. Some species, like the Plains spadefoot toad, can change into a froglet in just a few days. Usually, however, tadpoles need about one month to become froglets. Sometimes, females lay so many eggs in a small pool of water that the growing tadpoles run out of space and food. At these times, some of the tadpoles begin to eat each other, although they can recognize their littermates and do not gulp them down, too.

SPADEFOOT TOADS AND PEOPLE

People may hear these frogs occasionally during their mating season, but they rarely see the animals in the wild. Spadefoot toads are not especially popular in the pet trade, although some people do keep them in their homes. Nonetheless, at least one species has received attention. In 2003, the state government of New Mexico named the New Mexico Spadefoot Toad, a red and brown speckled species, as its official state amphibian.

CONSERVATION STATUS

The World Conservation Union (IUCN) considers one species to be Endangered, which means that it faces a very high risk of extinction in the wild. The U.S. Fish and Wildlife Services does not list any species as being at risk. The IUCN Endangered species is Varaldi's spadefoot toad, which lives in a few small areas in Morocco in northwestern Africa. Like many other spadefoot toads, it lives mainly underground in sandy soils, but comes on land to mate in puddles and pools of water. As humans farm in areas where the frog lives, the soil is beginning to pack down, which makes the frog's digging more difficult, and new pollutants are entering the watering holes. Both are likely hurting the frogs. In addition, some frogs are able to breed in larger ponds that are filled with water all year, but these ponds often are also home to fishes that eat the frogs.

Although no other species is considered to be at risk, some populations, including Couch's spadefoot toad, appear to be disappearing due to pollution and/or habitat destruction.

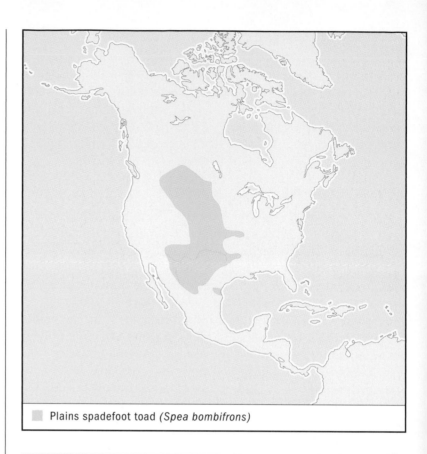

Plains spadefoot toad (*Spea bombifrons*)

PLAINS SPADEFOOT TOAD
Spea bombifrons

Physical characteristics: Plump and round-bodied, the Plains spadefoot toad has wrinkled skin. Its head has a short, rounded, and slightly upturned snout and two very large eyes with catlike, vertical pupils. Between its eyes and running down to the top of its snout is a blisterlike hump, also known as a boss. Its short forelegs end in feet with small toes that have no webbing between. It has webbed feet on its large back legs, and the bottom of each foot has a single, small, black scoop, or spade, below the toes. Its back is light tan, milk chocolate-colored, greenish brown, or gray, sometimes with four light-colored stripes running from head to rump, or with numerous faint, darker brown spots. The toads occasionally have red or yellow sand-like bumps on their backs, which may sit in small dark spots. The underside is white, although the males sometimes have a noticeable blue

or gray tint on the sides of the throat. Adults grow to about 1.5 to 2.5 inches (3.8 to 6.4 centimeters) from the tip of the snout to the end of the rump.

Geographic range: The Plains spadefoot toad is a North American species and lives from northern Mexico into the southern tip of Texas and in a wide area from northern Mexico through many central U.S. states and into southern Canada.

Habitat: It makes its home in the dry prairies and farm fields that are common in central North America.

Diet: Night hunters, adults eat insects and other invertebrates.

Behavior and reproduction: The Plains spadefoot toad is a fossorial (faw-SOR-ee-ul) animal, which means that it lives most of its life underground. The small spades on its feet help it dig hind-end-first into the loose, often sandy soil of its habitat. It leaves its burrows at night after a rain or when the air is humid to look for food. It also comes out of its underground burrow to mate. When the spring rains drench the land, hundreds of these frogs will all hop from their burrows at once to mate. Because so many frogs mate together over a short time, scientists call them explosive breeders. The males find small puddles and shallow ponds and begin making their squeaky calls to attract females. While mating, each female lays hundreds of eggs, which stick to underwater plants, rocks, and other objects. Within two days, the eggs hatch into tadpoles, and these change into froglets in as little as two weeks. This quick egg-to-tadpole-to-froglet growth is important, because they live in a habitat where puddles and ponds can dry up in a very short time. A tadpole cannot survive without water. Males and females may mate again later in the year if another heavy rain soaks the ground.

Plains spadefoot toads and people: People only notice this toad when a group of males is calling together.

Conservation status: This species is not considered to be threatened. In some areas, however, its habitat is disappearing at an alarming rate. A few states and provinces have now begun taking measures to protect it.   ■

FOR MORE INFORMATION

Books:

Duellman, William E., and Linda Trueb. *Biology of Amphibians.* Baltimore: Johns Hopkins University Press, 1994.

Halliday, Tim, and Kraig Adler, eds. *The Encyclopedia of Reptiles and Amphibians.* New York: Facts on File, 1991.

Stebbins, Robert C. *A Field Guide to Western Reptiles and Amphibians.* Boston: Houghton Mifflin, 1985.

Tyning, Thomas. *A Guide to Amphibians and Reptiles.* Boston: Little, Brown and Company, 1990.

Zug, George R., Laurie J. Vitt, and Janalee P. Caldwell. *Herpetology: An Introductory Biology of Amphibians and Reptiles.* 2nd ed. San Diego: Academic Press, 2001.

Periodicals:

Fellman, Bruce. "To eat or not to eat." *National Wildlife.* February-March 1995 (volume 33): page 42.

Freeman, Melanie. "The Spadefoot Toad." *Boy's Quest.* February-March 2002 (volume 7): page 2.

Web sites:

"Eastern Spadefoot Toad." *Connecticut Department of Environmental Protection.* http://dep.state.ct.us/burnatr/wildlife/factshts/esptoad.htm (accessed on February 14, 2005).

"Eastern Spadefoot Toad." *Savannah River Ecology Laboratory, University of Georgia.* http://www.uga.edu/srelherp/anurans/scahol.htm (accessed on February 14, 2005).

"Frogs and Toads Found in Texas." *Texas Parks and Wildlife.* http://www.tpwd.state.tx.us/nature/education/tracker/amphibians/species/ (accessed on February 14, 2005).

"Great Basin Spadefoot Toad." *B.C. Frogwatch Program, Ministry of Water, Land, and Air Protection, Government of British Columbia.* http://wlapwww.gov.bc.ca/wld/frogwatch/whoswho/factshts/spadeft.htm (accessed on February 14, 2005).

"Official State Amphibian: New Mexico Spadefoot Toad." *Netstate.com.* http://www.netstate.com/states/symb/amphibians/nm_spadefoot_toad.htm (accessed on February 14, 2005).

"Plains Spadefoot, *Spea bombifrons.*" *Northern Prairie Wildlife Research Center, U.S. Geological Survey.* http://www.npwrc.usgs.gov/narcam/idguide/speab.htm (accessed on February 14, 2005).

"Plains Spadefoot Toad." *Lee Richardson Zoo.* http://www.garden-city.org/zoo/animalinfo/plains_spadefoot.htm (accessed on February 14, 2005).

Class: Amphibia

Order: Anura

Family: Pelodytidae

Number of species: 3 species

family

C H A P T E R

PHYSICAL CHARACTERISTICS

Parsley frogs have little dark green blotches on their backs that look somewhat like pieces of parsley. Many people are familiar with parsley as the small, ruffled leaf that often decorates a plate of food at a restaurant. The frogs are rather thin and somewhat flattened with short, slender forelegs and long back legs. Their backs are brown, light greenish brown, or gray and speckled with small rounded warts. The Caucasus parsley frog, also known as the Caucasian parsley frog or Caucasian mud-diver, may have some red dots on its back. The underside in all three species is whitish to gray. The toes on their front feet are long and thin and have no webbing between them. The even-longer toes on the back feet have only a small amount of webbing. These frogs have large eyes with vertical pupils, a rounded snout, and no obvious eardrum on the side of the head. They are rather small frogs, growing to 1.8 to 2.2 inches (4.5 to 5.5 centimeters) long from snout to rump.

Males and females may be quite similar. In the Caucasus parsley frog, however, the female has a reddish back and lower belly. During mating season, the male parsley frog may develop small, rough pads on the toes of its front feet, on its forelegs, and/or on its chest. The rough spots, called nuptial (NUHP-shul) pads, help the male hold onto the wet and slippery body of the female during mating.

Until the year 2000, scientists thought that two of the three species in this family—the common parsley frog and the Iberian parsley frog—were the same species. The Iberian parsley frog, however, has some slight differences. Additional studies are now needed to find out whether populations that were thought to be common parsley frogs are actually Iberian parsley frogs and how the "new" species is surviving overall. In other research, scientists believe this family once had more than just three species. Based on fossils they have studied, they think the extinct species may actually outnumber the living ones.

Some people group the parsley frogs within the family spadefoot toads, but most scientists believe the parsley frogs should be separated into their own family as they are listed here.

GEOGRAPHIC RANGE

All three species of this family live in Europe and/or western Asia. The species known simply as the parsley frog or common parsley frog is found in southwestern Europe. The Caucasus parsley frog lives in Turkey and other areas near the Caspian Sea. The Iberian parsley frog lives in the southern parts of Portugal and Spain.

HABITAT

Parsley frogs live in various moist places, often near water. Some may live in forests near a stony stream, and others in a meadow near a pond. Tadpoles can survive in somewhat salty water.

DIET

Mostly night-feeders, the parsley frogs eat insects, worms, slugs, and other invertebrates (in-VER-teh-brehts), or animals without backbones.

BEHAVIOR AND REPRODUCTION

By day, parsley frogs take cover under rocks or in the bushes or grass that grow along walls. They leave their hiding places as the sun sets and begin hopping about looking for food. They usually stay fairly close to a body of water. If they feel threatened, they can either use their long, strong legs to leap out of sight on land or into the water, where they are good swimmers. The warts on their skin contain a bad-tasting poison, which is useful if a predator happens to catch and try to eat one.

When fall comes, some of the parsley frogs that live in colder areas prepare for hibernation (high-bur-NAY-shun), which is a state of deep sleep. They may start hibernating as early as

BIG BABIES

In some species, such as the parsley frogs, the tadpoles can be larger than the adults. How can this be? The answer is in the tail. As a tadpole changes into a froglet, it absorbs its tail. In other words, the tail disappears into the body. Often, new froglets still have small stumps of tail that have not yet vanished. In most frogs, tadpoles make the change into froglets when they are just a few months old. In parsley frogs and some other types of frogs, however, the tadpoles may not become froglets for one or two years. These especially old tadpoles can grow to be quite large—sometimes nearly twice as big as the adults.

September and not become active again until the following March. The Iberian parsley frog, which lives in the warmer climate of southern Spain and southern Portugal, remains active all year long and actually is the most lively in winter, when the cold-climate species are hibernating.

For cold-climate species, mating begins in the spring when warm rains soak the ground. In its much warmer climate, however, the Iberian parsley frog mates from fall to spring and becomes less active in the hot summer months. The males travel to ponds, puddles, and sometimes very slow-flowing streams and start calling. Scientists believe that they may call underwater. To mate, a male climbs onto female's back, and she lays her eggs. A female may lay several dozen eggs at a time and, depending on the species, may lay several hundred over the whole night. Sometimes, they may breed more than once a year, such as spring and fall. The eggs attach to sticks and leaves underwater and eventually hatch into tadpoles. Eggs of the Iberian parsley frog hatch quickly, needing just a week before the tadpoles wiggle out.

Depending on the species of parsley frog and the weather, the tadpoles may change into froglets about two to three months later, may hibernate as tadpoles and make the change the second year, or may hibernate yet again and change into froglets in their third year. Tadpoles hibernate by sinking into the mud at the bottom of their pond or pool of water and remaining there until the spring. Tadpoles that wait longer to change into froglets can grow quite large, sometimes even becoming bigger than the adults. Parsley frogs usually are old enough to have young of their own when they are two to three years old. Only frogs, and not tadpoles, can mate and have young.

PARSLEY FROGS AND PEOPLE

People rarely keep these frogs as pets, do not eat them as food, and do not collect them for experiments or for making medicines. Since parsley frogs spend their days hidden away, most people never see them. The frogs may still be helpful to humans, however, because they eat insects that some people consider pests.

CONSERVATION STATUS

None of these three species is generally considered to be at risk. However, several countries have listed them as Endangered or Vulnerable. An Endangered species faces a very high risk of extinction in the wild, and a Vulnerable species faces a high risk. In some populations, the number of frogs has dropped quite low. Often, the destruction of habitat is to blame. Sometimes, people drain water from a marsh or stream to turn it into farmland or to build homes or businesses. In addition, the habitat may become dangerous to frogs because of fertilizers and other pollutants that drain from human developments into streams and ponds.

Parsley frog (*Pelodytes punctatus*)

PARSLEY FROG
Pelodytes punctatus

Physical characteristics: Also known as the common parsley frog or mud-diver, adults of this species are thin, somewhat flattened frogs. They have brown, light brownish green, or gray backs with dark green blotches and have numerous, small warts. The belly and the throat are whitish, and the underside of their legs is yellow-colored. They have a thin, black stripe on each side of the head from the snout, through the middle of the eye, and to the foreleg, as well as dark blotches on the upper lip. Their eyes are large and copper-colored and have vertical pupils. They do not have obvious eardrums showing on the sides of the head. Their forelegs are smaller and thinner than their hind legs, and all four limbs are brown with green blotches. The parsley frog has long toes. The toes on the front feet have no

webbing between them, and the toes on the back feet have only a little webbing at the bottom. Adults grow to 1.4 to 1.8 inches (3.5 to 4.5 centimeters) from the tip of the snout to the end of the rump. The tadpole is greenish brown with noticeable dark eyes. It has an oval-shaped head and body and a long tail. Tadpoles can reach 1.6 to 2.6 inches (4 to 6.5 centimeters) long from head to tail before they change into froglets.

Geographic range: The common parsley frog lives in southwestern Europe, including Belgium, Luxembourg, France, Italy, Spain, and Portugal.

Habitat: The common parsley frog lives in many habitats, including forests, shrubby woods, and farmland, that either have very damp ground or are near a pond or stream. They mate in streams and small ponds.

Diet: It eats insects and other small invertebrates.

Behavior and reproduction: During the day, these frogs hide under stones or in small dips or holes in the ground, but they sometimes will venture out during or after a good rain. They become active from dusk to dawn. Animals that are active only at sunup and sundown are crepuscular (kreh-PUSS-kyoo-ler). Animals active at night are called nocturnal (nahk-TER-nuhl). Using these terms, the parsley frog is both crepuscular and nocturnal. The parsley frogs that live in warmer areas are active almost all year long. Those that live in cooler areas may survive the winter by hibernating. Some hibernate from October to February or March.

When outside from dawn to dusk, the frogs protect themselves from predators in several ways. The colors of the back and head help blend them into the background and make them less noticeable to predators. If a predator does approach them on land, however, they are excellent jumpers and can often leap away. When they are near the water, they will jump in and swim. Although their hind feet do not have much webbing to help boost them through the water, they are still good swimmers. If a predator happens to catch a parsley frog, the warts in its skin ooze a mild poison that may taste bad enough to convince the predator to leave the frog alone.

Their mating season usually begins in the spring, but if the weather is right, they may mate almost any time of year, including the summer and fall. The male's call sounds a bit like a heavy, old door quietly creaking open. Females lay about 50 to 100 eggs at a time and may lay as many as 1,000 to 1,600 eggs a year in small strings or clumps. The eggs are tiny and brown and coated with a thick, see-through gel. The eggs stick to underwater plants and stems and hatch into tadpoles that may grow to be larger than the adult frogs.

Parsley frogs and people: Like most other frogs, this species eats insects that people may consider pests.

Conservation status: This species is not generally considered to be at risk, but Belgium, France, and other countries have listed it as Endangered or Vulnerable. In these areas, the numbers of parsley frogs have declined because of habitat destruction, especially the draining of water.   ■

FOR MORE INFORMATION

Books:

Arnold, E. Nicholas. *Reptiles and Amphibians of Europe (Princeton Field Guides)*. Princeton, NJ: Princeton University Press, 2003.

Arnold, E. N., J. A. Burton, and D. W. Ovenden. *Reptiles and Amphibians of Britain & Europe (Collins Field Guide)*. London: HarperCollins, 1999.

Duellman, William E., and Linda Trueb. *Biology of Amphibians*. Baltimore: Johns Hopkins University Press, 1994.

Halliday, Tim, and Kraig Adler, eds. *The Encyclopedia of Reptiles and Amphibians.* New York: Facts on File, 1991.

Zug, George R., Laurie J. Vitt, and Janalee P. Caldwell. *Herpetology.* 2nd edition. San Diego: Academic Press, 2001.

Web sites:

"Dramatic Declines for European Amphibians." IUCN press release. http://www.countdown2010.net/documents/european%20frog%20an d%20toad-2.pdf (accessed on February 14, 2005).

Heying, H. "Pelodytidae" *Animal Diversity Web.* http://animaldiversity .ummz.umich.edu/site/accounts/information/Pelodytidae.html (accessed on February 14, 2005).

"Iberian Parsley Frog." *Amphibians and Reptiles of Europe.* http://www .herp.it/indexjs.htm?SpeciesPages/PelodIberi.htm (accessed on February 14, 2005).

"Parsley Frog, Common Parsley Frog, Mud-diver." *Amphibians and Reptiles of Europe.* http://www.herp.it/indexjs.htm?SpeciesPages/ PelodPunct.htm (accessed on February 14, 2005).

Class: Amphibia

Order: Anura

Family: Heleophrynidae

Number of species: 6 species

family

CHAPTER

phylum

class

subclass

order

monotypic order

suborder

▲ family

PHYSICAL CHARACTERISTICS

With colors and patterns that almost perfectly match the forest floor where they live, the ghost frogs live up to their name and, when they are very still, seem to vanish into the background. The Cape ghost frog, also known as Purcell's ghost frog, has a brown back and head that are covered with black blotches—almost as if someone had shaken out a wet paintbrush and splattered black paint on the frog. When in its habitat where the green mosses and plants and dark clumps of dirt and pebbles form a patterned blanket on the ground, the frog blends in well enough almost to disappear. People and predators can walk within a few feet of this frog and never notice it.

The other five species of ghost frog also have such camouflage, or cryptic (CRIP-tik) coloration. The frogs may be tan, brown, purplish brown, gray, or green, usually have darker blotches on the back and head, and may have dark bands around the front and back legs. The blotches may be purple, brown, or nearly black. The Natal ghost frog has the opposite coloration with a brown to black head and back and yellowish to green markings. The ghost frogs' undersides are typically lighter colored and almost see-through, giving them another ghost-like quality. Sometimes they have dark markings on the throat.

All ghost frogs have front and back toes that end in large, triangle-shaped pads. They have long, thin hind legs and shorter front legs on bodies that are slightly flattened. Their back toes are webbed, sometimes all the way to the tips. Their large, bulging eyes have catlike, vertical pupils, and their snouts are rounded in front and somewhat flattened overall. In their mouths, the tongue is disk-shaped, and small teeth line only the upper jaw.

Ghost frogs are small- to medium-sized frogs, reaching 1.4 to at least 2.6 inches (3.5 to 6.5 centimeters) long from the tip of the snout to the rump. Males and females look mostly alike, but the females usually are larger. Females of the largest species sometimes reach lengths a bit longer than 2.6 inches (6.5 centimeters). Males of the species called Rose's ghost frog also have small black spines on their lower front and rear legs, back, and thighs, and male Natal ghost frogs develop pads on the lower front legs and little spines on the toes of their front feet during breeding season.

The ghost frogs were once grouped in another family that includes the Surinam horned frog and other leptodactylid frogs, but they now have their own family. Although scientists believe that the ghost frogs are a very ancient group, they have not yet found any fossils of species in this family.

GEOGRAPHIC RANGE

Ghost frogs live in and around South Africa's Drakensberg Mountains, where some of the world's highest waterfalls are found.

HABITAT

The ghost frogs may make their homes among the forests and sometimes grasslands of the Drakensberg mountain range, which are the highest mountains in South Africa. They can be found from sea level up the mountains' steep slopes to 9,843 feet (3,000 meters), but usually in an area with a swift, rocky river or stream, which is where they mate and have their young.

DIET

The adult diet includes various insects, snails, and other invertebrates (in-VER-teh-brehts), or animals with no backbone, as well as smaller frogs. They apparently are not cannibalistic (can-ih-bull-ISS-tik), which means that they do not eat members of their own species. The tadpoles are vegetarians and eat algae (AL-jee) that they scrape off underwater rocks. Algae are plantlike growths that live in water but have no true roots, leaves, or stems.

BEHAVIOR AND REPRODUCTION

During the day, they hide from sight under or between rocks, or in cracks within rocks. Their flattened bodies help them to squeeze into even small openings. At night, they hop out to look for food. Their sticky, wide front and back toe tips help them to climb easily up even the wet and slippery sides of streamside rocks. Predators often do not see these camouflaged frogs, but even when they do, they often leave them alone, because the frog's skin contains a mild poison that many predators learn to avoid.

In the breeding season, the skin on these frogs becomes baggy. They usually breed from spring to mid-summer after the heavy storms of the rainy season. Male ghost frogs group together at waterfalls or at a river or stream with a fast current and begin calling from a hiding place under a rock or in a rock crack or from a spot that is sprinkled with water from a waterfall. Some species call both day and night, but others call mostly at night. Depending on the species, the call may be quite loud or so quiet that it can only be heard from about 10 feet (3 meters) away. Some calls, like those of the Cape ghost frogs and Natal ghost frogs, are repeating ringing sounds. Male and female ghost frogs are excellent swimmers and spend much of the breeding season in the water.

The females lay their 50 to 200 eggs one at a time either in a slow part of the stream or river or in a puddle or other wet area alongside the river or stream. Some species attach their large and gel-covered eggs to the bottom of an underwater rock. After the eggs are deposited, the female and male leave, and the eggs and tadpoles develop on their own. Usually within a week, the eggs hatch into tadpoles, which may stay in the quiet water or move into faster flowing water. They use their suction-cup-shaped mouths to grab onto rocks, while they scrape algae from them with tiny teeth. The tadpoles typically change into froglets when they are 1 to 2 years old.

GHOST FROGS AND PEOPLE

People rarely see these frogs.

CONSERVATION STATUS

According to the World Conservation Union (IUCN), two of the six species are Critically Endangered, which means that they face an extremely high risk of extinction in the wild. One is Hewitt's ghost frog, which lives in and around four streams about 1,310 to 1,805 feet (400 to 550 meters) above sea level in the Elandsberg mountains of South Africa's Eastern Cape Province. The frog breeds in the streams, but spends the rest of the year in the surrounding areas that have scattered trees and shrubs. Fires and human activity, like the logging of the few trees and the building of roads are destroying the frog's nonbreeding habitat and also allowing more dirt to drain into the streams where the frog has its young. In addition, new fish species that eat the frogs have been added to the streams, and in some places, the streams have dried up.

The other Critically Endangered species is Rose's ghost frog, which is also known as the Table Mountain ghost frog or thumbed ghost frog. This species makes its home in mountain forests, shrubby areas, and even inside caves on the sides of Table Mountain between 785 and 3,480 feet (240 to 1,060 meters) above sea level. The entire area where it lives is inside the Cape Peninsula National Park. New plants in the park, numerous park visitors, and a high number of fires are changing the frog's habitat and making it difficult for this species to survive. In addition, people have built holding areas for some of the mountain water, which is taking some away from the streams where the frogs' eggs and tadpoles develop. Since the tadpoles need more than a year before they turn into frogs and can leave the streams, they may die if too much water is sidetracked for the holding areas.

To learn more about the frogs of South Africa and how well they are surviving, scientists are now collecting information about them through the Southern African Frog Atlas Project (SAFAP).

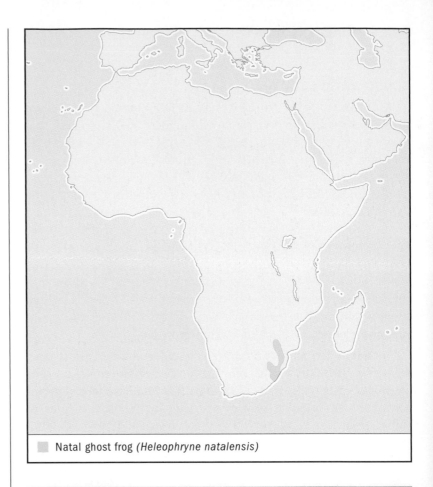

■ Natal ghost frog (*Heleophryne natalensis*)

SPECIES
ACCOUNT

NATAL GHOST FROG
Heleophryne natalensis

Physical characteristics: The Natal ghost frog has a brown to black head and back with yellowish to green blotches, and a lighter colored underside with markings on its throat. Like other ghost frogs, its body is flattened a bit, and it has small triangular-shaped pads on the tips of its front and back toes. Its large, bulging eyes have vertical, cat-like pupils.

Geographic range: It lives in the Drakensberg and Maluti mountains of South Africa, Lesotho, and Swaziland from 1,900 to 8,776 feet (580 to 2,675 meters) above sea level.

   Grzimek's Student Animal Life Resource

Habitat: The forests and sometimes the grasslands of the eastern mountains of southern Africa are home to these frogs. As the breeding season draws near, they travel 0.6 miles (1 kilometer) or more to reach a fast-moving stream where they mate and have their young.

Diet: Tadpoles are vegetarian and scrape algae from rocks with their small teeth. As adults, Natal ghost frogs eat spiders, small insects, and other invertebrates.

Behavior and reproduction: These frogs usually hide in holes along stream banks and cliffs during the daytime, but sometimes venture out to waterfalls, where they sit in water-splashed areas and look for things to eat. They are most active at night, however, and do the bulk of their hunting then. Their breeding season begins after the heavy spring rains. During this time, the males begin calling from hideaways under rocks, or in plants near a stream, or in the splashing water from a nearby waterfall. Their call sounds like the repeated ringing of a small, quiet bell. The females arrive, mate with the males, and lay their eggs beneath underwater rocks. In about four or five days, the eggs hatch into tadpoles. The tadpoles turn into froglets when they are 2 years old.

Natal ghost frogs and people: People rarely see this frog.

Conservation status: While the World Conservation Union (IUCN) does not list this rather common frog as being at risk, it does note that the frog's numbers are slowly dropping. It believes several things are to blame. First, loggers and/or farmers are cutting down the forests that are home to this species. The removal of the trees can also muddy up the streams and rivers and make it difficult for the frogs to breed there. This muddying happens because plants, including trees, help keep rain from quickly washing down hills and slopes and taking the soil with it into the water. In addition, people are draining away water from under the ground. People are also putting barriers, or dams, in the rivers. Both activities can cause the levels of the rivers and streams to fall. If too much water disappears, the tadpoles, which need water to survive, could die. Another threat comes from fish, such as trout, that people put in the rivers. People may add trout to a waterway for sport fishing or for food. The problem is that the trout eat many other animals, including tadpoles and frogs. ■

FOR MORE INFORMATION

Books:

Channing, A. *Amphibians of Central and Southern Africa.* Ithaca, NY: Cornell University Press, 2001.

Halliday, Tim, and Kraig Adler, eds. *The Encyclopedia of Reptiles and Amphibians (Smithsonian Handbooks).* New York: Facts on File, 1991.

Miller, Sara Swan. *Frogs and Toads: The Leggy Leapers.* New York: Franklin Watts, 2000.

Web sites:

"Cape Ghost Frog." *Cape Nature Conservation.* http://www.capenature. org.za/cederbergproject/html/capeghost.html (accessed on February 17, 2005).

"The Ghost Family: Six Amphibians Exclusive to Southern Africa." *The World Conservation Union (IUCN).* http://www.iucnrosa.org.zw/news/ ghost_frogs.html (accessed on February 17, 2005).

Heying, H. "Heleophrynidae." *Animal Diversity Web.* http://animaldiversity. ummz.umich.edu/site/accounts/information/Heleophrynidae.html (accessed on February 17, 2005).

"Table Mountain Ghost Frog." *University of the Western Cape.* http://www.botany.uwc.ac.za/envfacts/fynbos/ghost_frog.htm (accessed on February 17, 2005).

"UCT (University of Cape Town) scientists join project." *Amphibian Conservation Alliance.* http://www.frogs.org/news/article.asp?CategoryID= 46&InfoResourceID=939 (accessed on February 17, 2005).

family

CHAPTER

PHYSICAL CHARACTERISTICS

A small family, the Seychelles frogs include only four species. They are Gardiner's frog, which is one of the tiniest frogs in the world; a species known simply as Seychelles frog; Thomasset's frog; and the family's newest member, Seychelles palm frog, which scientists named in 2002. The frogs have a typical frog appearance with hind legs that are longer than the front legs, long toes on the hind feet and shorter ones on the front feet, and large, bulging eyes on the head. They also have a somewhat pointy snout and horizontal pupils in their eyes.

The four species come in different colors. The upper body of the Seychelles frog is usually yellowish brown with black spots and blotches. The Gardiner's frog may be reddish brown or tan with or without spots or stripes and sometimes with noticeable, small warts. The newly named Seychelles palm frog is light brown with a dark, diamond-shaped pattern in the middle of its back and faded dark patterns on its hind legs. Finally, Thomasset's frog is dark brown to reddish brown with a thin, light stripe running from its snout down the middle of its slightly warty back to its rump. The back also sometimes has small light-colored specks on either side of the line. Whatever their color or pattern, however, the four species blend in quite well with their habitat. Males and females look alike.

Depending on the species, the adults may be very small or medium-sized. The Gardiner's frog, which is tiny enough to completely fit on a U.S. dime, only reaches about 0.4 to 0.5 inch (1.0 to 1.3 centimeters) long from the tip of its slightly

phylum

class

subclass

order

monotypic order

suborder

▲ **family**

pointy snout to the end of its rump. The largest member of the family is Thomasset's frog. This species usually grows to 1.8 inches (4.5 centimeters) in length. As in many other types of frogs, the females of each species are a bit larger than the males. For example, a female Gardiner's frog usually grows to 0.47 inch (1.19 centimeters) long and sometimes reaches 0.5 inch (1.3 centimeters) long, while the male typically grows to 0.4 inch (1 centimeter) long with a maximum length of 0.43 inch (1.1 centimeters).

In 2003, scientists announced the discovery of a new species of frog, known only by its scientific name—*Nasikabatrachus sahyadrensis*. They placed this species in its own family, but have since decided that its nearest relatives are the Seychelles frogs. In other words, the new species and the Seychelles frogs have the same ancestors. *Nasikabatrachus sahyadrensis* is a very odd-looking purple frog that apparently stays underground for all but two weeks a year, when it comes out to mate. The World Conservation Union (IUCN) considers it to be Endangered, or facing a very high risk of extinction in the wild, because it lives in a small area of mountain forests, and its habitat is disappearing as the forest is turned into farmland. As of 2004, scientists had only found 135 individuals, and only three of those were females.

GEOGRAPHIC RANGE

Seychelles frogs live only in the country called Seychelles, which is a group of islands in the western Indian Ocean about 580 miles (930 kilometers) northeast of Madagascar. Scientists believe that these islands may have been part of India far in the past, but about 55 to 65 million years ago, India began to slowly move away to its current location, about 1,800 miles (2,900 kilometers) north and now part of Asia. Like many other islands, the Seychelles islands are actually the tops of mountains that are mostly underwater. Scientists believe that the common ancestor of the Seychelles frogs and the new species of *Nasikabatrachus sahyadrensis*, lived more than 130 million years ago when Seychelles and India were still connected. As of yet, they have found no fossils of any of the four Seychelles frogs or of the new purple species.

HABITAT

Within Seychelles, these frogs live only on Mahé and Silhouette islands, and usually more than 656 feet (200 meters) above sea level, although a single Thomasset's frog was found lower on the mountain, at about 312 feet (95 meters) above sea level. Rainforests are home for all four species. The Seychelles palm frog only lives in those areas that have plenty of palms, and Thomasset's frog likes to remain in forests near rocky streams.

DIET

They will eat mosquitoes, fruit flies, and other small insects, as well as mites and other invertebrates (in-VER-teh-brehts), which are animals without backbones, that they find in the forest. Thomasset's frog also hunts for insects alongside streams.

BEHAVIOR AND REPRODUCTION

The four Seychelles frogs usually stay out of sight under piles of leaves lying on the rainforest floor, inside cracks in rocks, and even within hollow plant stems or on the base of a leaf where it attaches to a stem. The Seychelles palm frog, for example, hunkers down in the leaves of palm and sometimes banana trees. Usually, only rains will bring the Seychelles frogs out of their hiding places. During these wet periods, the frogs will hop about day or night looking for food. Thomasset's frog often settles on a stream-side rock after sunset and waits for flying insects to zip by closely enough for it to capture and eat them.

NEW PURPLE FROG!

In 2003, scientists announced the discovery of a new, red-eyed, purple frog that is so unusual, they even created a separate family for it. The frog, which is only known by its scientific name—*Nasikabatrachus sahyadrensis*—was described in *National Geographic News* as "a bloated doughnut with stubby legs and a pointy snout." Villagers in a small village in western India found the odd frog while digging a well and turned the purple creature over to scientists. After studying it, the scientists agreed that it was not only a new species, but was so different that it needed its own family, which is now known as Nasikabatrachidae. Of all the other frogs in the world, they think it is most closely related to the Seychelles frogs, which live 1,900 miles (3,000 kilometers) away on an island country in the Indian Ocean.

The mating season occurs during the rainy season. Males may call during the day or at night from under leaves or from one of their other hiding spots. Unlike the males of many other types of frogs, males in the Seychelles frog family do their calling alone and from their own personal, on-land location. In other frogs, the males often group together in one place—usually in the water—and all call at the same time.

From the "wrracck toc toc toc toc" of the Thomasset's frog to the high "peep" of the Gardiner's frog, each species has its own call. To mate, the male climbs onto the female's back and uses his front legs to hang just in front of her hind legs. Although scientists do not know how some of these frogs lay their eggs or how those eggs develop into frogs, they do have details about Gardiner's frog and the Seychelles frog species. The female Gardiner's frog lays her eight to 15 eggs in a hiding place on the ground and stays with them. Instead of hatching into tadpoles, these eggs hatch in three to four weeks right into tiny froglets, each one about 0.12 inch (3 millimeters) long—no bigger than a grain of rice. As the froglets hop away, the female's job is done and she leaves. In the Seychelles frog species, the female lays her eggs on land and stays with them just as the Gardiner's frog does, but her eggs hatch in two to three weeks into tadpoles. Without water to swim in, the tadpoles instead wiggle up and cling to the mother's back. They stay there until a short while after they turn into froglets, and finally hop off to live on their own.

As yet, scientists are not sure how Thomasset's frogs or the Seychelles palm frogs mate, where the females lay their eggs, whether their eggs develop into tadpoles or right into froglets, and if the adult female or adult male watch over their young. They do know, however, that the female Thomasset's frog lays large eggs, and they think this may mean that her eggs skip the tadpole stage and hatch right into froglets. All frog species with eggs that hatch into tadpoles go through what is known as indirect development. Those whose eggs skip the tadpole phase and develop directly into froglets go through direct development.

SEYCHELLES FROGS AND PEOPLE

People rarely see these secretive frogs.

CONSERVATION STATUS

According to the World Conservation Union (IUCN), all four species are Vulnerable, which means that they face a high risk of extinction in the wild. Because all these frogs live in small areas, and some have small populations, changes to their habitat could possibly be dangerous to them. Fortunately, many live in Morne Seychellois National Park or inside the boundaries of a conservation project on Silhouette Island, and some seem to be able to survive in newly growing forests that were once cut down.

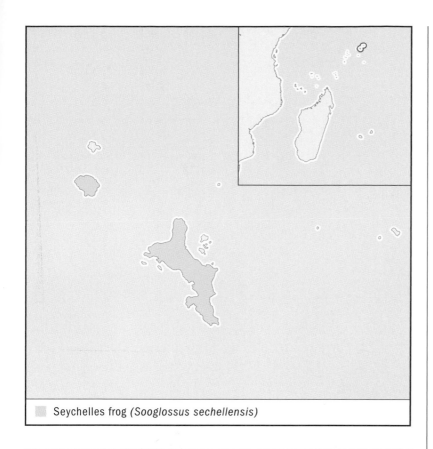

Seychelles frog (*Sooglossus sechellensis*)

SEYCHELLES FROG
Sooglossus sechellensis

Physical characteristics: The Seychelles frog is yellowish-brown with black spots and blotches on its head, legs, and back. The blotches on its back legs may look like bands. It usually has a triangular-shaped, dark spot that runs from one of its rather large eyes across its forehead to the other eye. Its snout is somewhat pointed. The toes on its long hind legs and shorter, thinner front legs have no webbing between them. The females usually grow to about 0.8 inch (2 centimeters) long from the tip of the snout to the end of the rump, while the typical size of the males is about 0.6 inch (1.5 centimeters).

Geographic range: Seychelles frogs live on Mahé and Silhouette Islands in Seychelles, a country in the Indian Ocean.

Habitat: They make their homes in the rainforests of the island mountains at least 660 feet (200 meters) above sea level. They usually hide in leaf piles on the ground, often in areas where cinnamon grows.

Diet: Seychelles frogs' diet includes small insects and other invertebrates that the frogs find on the forest floor.

Behavior and reproduction: They usually remain hidden, except on wet days and nights. During these rainy periods, they hop out of their hiding spots to search for food. To mate, the males begin calling from under the leaves at any hour of the day or night. A male climbs onto the back of a female and mates with her while hanging onto her body just above her hind limbs. She lays her eggs on land, and her six to 15 eggs hatch into tadpoles, which scramble onto her back. The tadpoles stay on her back and soon turn into froglets. The froglets leave her back to grow up on their own. At one time, scientists thought that the tadpoles rode on the back of an adult male. A closer look, however, showed that it was the female who was the caretaker of her young.

Seychelles frogs and people: People rarely see these frogs.

Conservation status: According to the World Conservation Union (IUCN), this species is Vulnerable, which means that it faces a high risk of extinction in the wild. The frog lives in a small area on only two islands, but it is quite common there. Some of the frogs live in Morne Seychellois National Park and others within the boundaries of a conservation project on Silhouette Island. While it is doing quite well, a change to its habitat could possibly hurt some populations or the entire species. As people move closer to its habitat, conservationists are keeping a watchful eye on this species.   ■

FOR MORE INFORMATION

Books:

Halliday, Tim, and Kraig Adler, eds. *The Encyclopedia of Reptiles and Amphibians (Smithsonian Handbooks).* New York: Facts on File, 1991.

Noble, Gladwyn K. *The Biology of the Amphibia.* New York: McGraw-Hill, 1931.

Nussbaum, R. A. "Amphibians of the Seychelles." In *Biogeography and Ecology of the Seychelles Islands,* edited by D. R. Stoddart. Hague: Dr. W. Junk, 1984.

Periodicals:

"'Weird stuff' found in India." *Current Science* January 16, 2004 (89): 12.

Web sites:

"Amphibians." *Silhouette Island.* http://www.silhouette-island.com/public/amphibians.htm (accessed on February 22, 2005).

"The Animal Life." *Virtual Seychelles, Republic of Seychelles.* http://www.virtualseychelles.sc/envi/envi_nathis_frm.htm?nathis_body=envi_nathis_amph.htm (accessed on February 22, 2005).

"Pictures of Seychellfrogs (Sooglossidae)." *Swiss Herp.* http://www.swissherp.org/Amphibians/Sooglossidae/Sooglossidae.html (accessed on February 22, 2005).

family

CHAPTER

PHYSICAL CHARACTERISTICS

Although some scientists still believe that the Australian frogs should be divided up differently, this book follows the most common arrangement with two families: the 48 species of Australian ground frogs in the family Limnodynastidae and the 121 species of Australian toadlets and water frogs in the family Myobatrachidae. This entry deals with the Australian ground frogs.

Many of the Australian ground frogs have earth-tone colors, like brown, greenish brown, tan, and gray, often with spots, blotches, or other patterns that camouflage them against the dirt and plants of the ground. They commonly have lighter colored bellies, sometimes with faint patterns on the throat. Some species, however, are quite brightly colored. The northern banjo frog, which is also known as the scarlet-sided pobblebonk, has bright yellow sides with red and orange splashes of color under its legs, and the crucifix (or Catholic) toad has a warty, yellow back centered with a thick, dark brown, cross.

Some of the Australian ground frogs, like Fletcher's frog and the giant barred frog, have a typical frog shape with long, jumping hind legs and a large head. Others, like Spencer's burrowing frog and the sand frog, have shorter hind limbs and a blunter face more associated with toads. Most of the Australian ground frogs have little or no webbing on their front or rear toes.

The different species come in a variety of sizes. The smallest grow only to 0.9 inches (2.2 centimeters) long from the tip of the snout to the end of the rump, while others can reach as much as 4.3 inches (10.8 centimeters) long. Males and females usually look much alike, but in some species, the males develop very noticeable pads on their front toes and front legs during the breeding season. Called nuptial (NUHP-shul) pads, they help the male grab hold of the female during mating.

GEOGRAPHIC RANGE

Australian ground frogs are found in Australia and much of New Guinea.

HABITAT

Many of the species in this family are burrowers and live part of their lives underground. The giant burrowing frog is an example. During the daytime, and also during long, dry periods, this species uses its powerful hind legs to dig backward into the soil and bury itself. This behavior hides the frog from would-be predators and also helps to keep its skin moist. Other species in this family, like the woodworker frog and striped marsh frog, do not burrow. Instead, the woodworker frog hides in the cracks of rocks or in caves, and the striped marsh frog slips among the tall plants of the marshes, grasslands, and forests where it lives. The typical Australian ground frog mates in a stream or pond—sometimes one that dries up later in the year.

DIET

Australian ground frogs eat various types of invertebrates (in-VER-teh-brehts), which are animals without backbones, by either grasping them with a flick of the tongue or by biting at them. Australian ground frogs wait to hunt until night, and some do their hunting only after heavy rains soak the ground. In many species, such as the Baw Baw frog, the tadpoles do not need to search for food. Instead, they live on a sack of nutritious yolk that is left over from the egg and is still a part of their bodies.

BEHAVIOR AND REPRODUCTION

The species in this family are either nocturnal (nahk-TER-nuhl), which means that they are active mostly at night, or crepuscular (creh-PUS-kyuh-lur), which means that they come out only at dawn and dusk. As with the majority of other nocturnal or crepuscular frogs, the Australian ground frogs do not

KICKSTARTING LIFE

Giant barred frogs have an odd start to their lives. The female lays her eggs in the water with her back pointing toward the shore. As the eggs drop, she gives them a swift kick with her hind foot, flinging the gel-covered eggs in a splash of water onto shore where the eggs stick to the bank and shore-side rocks. When the tadpoles hatch from the eggs, they plop down into the water and swim off.

like air that is too dry, as it often is during the day. Instead, they come out when the air starts to become moister, which typically happens at night when the sun is down and the temperature starts to cool off. In addition, many Australian ground frogs will not even venture out at night during especially dry periods. For some of them, such dry periods, called droughts (drowts), happen at least once a year and may last several months. During this time, some of the Australian ground frogs burrow underground to keep from drying out.

Frogs must keep their skin moist to breathe. Like humans and other mammals, frogs can breathe through the nose and lungs. However, frogs also get a great deal of their oxygen right through the skin. If the skin dries out, they can no longer breathe through the skin, and they can suffocate. Many of the burrowing frogs in this family dig into the ground by swishing their powerful hind limbs one at a time and backing into the soil as their body wiggles back and forth. Other species, like Spencer's burrowing frog, dig backward into the soil, but turn their bodies in circles while they are doing it. These frogs look as if they are screwing themselves into the ground. Several species can stay underground for a number of months. They enter a sleep-like state, called estivation (es-tih-VAY-shun), and only wake up and become active again when the heavy spring rains drench the land. The tusked frog is an example. This animal, as well as numerous other members of this family, lives underground inside a cocoon of shed skin for several months each year.

Spring rains begin the mating season for most of the burrowing Australian ground frogs. In some of these species, all mating for the year is done within a few weeks' time. Some types of Australian ground frogs breed during certain seasons of the year, and others, like the spotted marsh frog, can mate and lay eggs all year long if the weather is right. Whenever their mating season begins, the males start calling at dusk or at night, usually from ponds, streams, or marshes, but sometimes from on land. Their calls attract females and also keep other males from invading their space. Different species have different calls.

The spotted marsh frog, for instance, calls with a repeated clicking noise of "tik-tik-tik"; the giant burrowing frog sometimes goes by the name of eastern owl frog, because its call of "oo-oo-oo-oo-oo" sounds like an owl hooting; and the common spadefoot frog has a knocking trill for its call.

Some of the females in this family lay their jelly-coated eggs in the water, often in a foamy nest. The female typically makes the foam by flailing her feet and whipping up her eggs and the mucus surrounding them. This adds air to the mixture and creates the foam. The eggs hatch into tadpoles, which then swim out into the water, or in some cases, stay in the foam until they turn into froglets. Other females lay their eggs in a foam nest, but make it inside a burrow or among plant leaves and branches on shore. When heavy rains flood the nest, the eggs hatch into tadpoles, which then live in the water.

AUSTRALIAN GROUND FROGS AND PEOPLE

Because many of these species burrow or otherwise stay out of sight during the day, people rarely see them. For some people who live in the deserts of Australia, however, a few of the burrowing species can be a good source of water. They dig up the frogs, whose bodies are plump with stored water, and suck the liquid from the frogs. Besides this unusual use, scientists are also now studying the slime of some species perhaps to make medicines.

CONSERVATION STATUS

According to the World Conservation Union (IUCN), one species is Critically Endangered, which means that it faces an extremely high risk of extinction in the wild, and seven others are Endangered, which means that they face a very high risk of extinction in the wild. In addition, IUCN lists two species as being Vulnerable and facing a high risk of extinction in the wild, one species as Near Threatened and at risk of becoming threatened with extinction in the future, and two species as Data Deficient, which means not enough information is available to make a judgment about the threat of extinction.

The Critically Endangered species is the Baw Baw frog, a dark-brown, warty creature that grows to about 2 inches long. It lives in tunnels in wetlands or under cover alongside streams in a small location on the Baw Baw Plateau, which lies in an area east of Melbourne. Although part of its habitat is inside the Baw

Baw National Park, the frog's numbers have dropped from more than 10,000 individuals in 1985 to fewer than 250 adults in 2004. Scientists are unsure exactly what is causing the Baw Baw frogs to disappear, but they think that dangers may come from a warming climate, infection with a type of fungus, pollution, or an increase in ultraviolet radiation. The sun gives off light in different forms, such as the light humans can see and other types they cannot, like ultraviolet, or UV, radiation. UV radiation is especially strong high in the mountains, which is where the Baw Baw frog lives. Through various experiments, scientists have learned that UV radiation causes death in the tadpoles of other mountain-living frogs and think the same thing may be happening to the Paw Paw frogs. Scientists are continuing to study this species to find out why it is vanishing.

The Endangered species are Fleay's barred frog, the giant barred frog, the red and yellow mountain frog, Loveridge's frog, the mountain frog, the sphagnum frog, and one known only by its scientific name of *Philoria pughi*. They all live in small areas, and often their habitat is being destroyed or changed by such activities as logging, movements of cattle that can trample the frogs' foam nests, and the building of homes, businesses, and roads. At least some Fleay's barred frogs have also died as a result of infection with a fungus. On the bright side, most of these frogs now live inside reserves or other protected areas, which should limit some of the dangers they face.

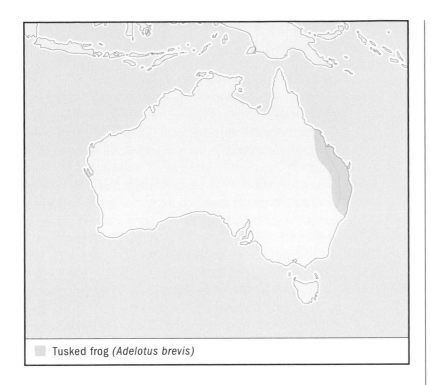

Tusked frog (*Adelotus brevis*)

TUSKED FROG
Adelotus brevis

Physical characteristics: The tusked frog gets its name from the male's two, unusually large, lower teeth, or tusks. The tusks only show if the frog's mouth is open. Otherwise, they are hidden inside. The female either has very small tusks or none at all. From above, the frog is tan with olive, brown, or black blotches on its back and markings that form broken band patterns on its legs. A reddish brown, somewhat triangular-shaped patch covers most of its snout. It has large eyes with horizontal pupils, and its front and hind feet have just a bit of webbing. Once the frog is flipped over, its color changes. The underside is mottled with black and white, and its legs are trimmed in dark orange or red. Unlike most other frogs, in which the males and females are the same size or the females are larger, male tusked frogs are usually the bigger of the two. Males typically grow to 1.3 to 1.7 inches (3.4 to 4.4 centimeters) from snout to rump, but females only reach 1.1 to 1.5 inches (2.9 to 3.8 centimeters) long. In addition, the male's head is larger than that of the female.

Geographic range: Tusked frogs live in the far eastern part of Australia from Queensland to New South Wales.

Habitat: Tusked frogs live in forests and sometimes in grasslands. The males usually stay near water, which may be a stream or just a puddle, but the females prefer drier places.

Diet: Their diet includes snails, insects, and other invertebrates. The males, which tend to live closer to the water, eat more snails, while the forest-living females eat invertebrates they find in their drier habitat.

Behavior and reproduction: Adults tend to stay under leaves and pieces of bark lying on the ground or huddled in some other hiding spot. During the breeding season, the males set up territories and defend them by biting other males with their long tusks. The bites can be severe and may leave scars. Each male calls from his territory with a voice that is a slow, soft "cluck - cluck - cluck." The female lays her eggs on the surface of the water in a foamy nest. The male stays with the nest, which is usually hidden from view under plants or other cover. The eggs, which measure less than 0.08 inches (2 millimeters) in diameter, hatch into tadpoles before changing into froglets.

Tusked frogs and people: People rarely see this frog in the wild or in the pet trade.

Conservation status: According to the World Conservation Union (IUCN), this species is Near Threatened, which means that it is at risk of becoming threatened with extinction in the future. Its numbers have dropped in many areas because of habitat loss, mainly as humans have turned the frogs' home into farmland or housing developments, and also because of infection with a fungus that is harming many species of frogs worldwide. ■

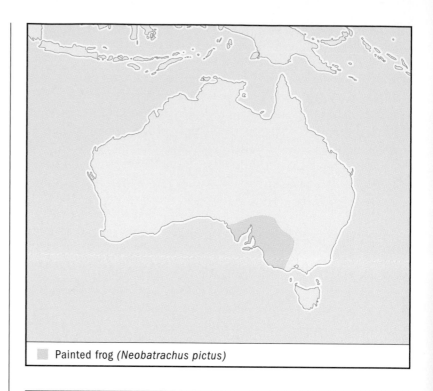

Painted frog *(Neobatrachus pictus)*

PAINTED FROG
Neobatrachus pictus

Physical characteristics: Also known as the painted burrowing frog, the painted frog is tan, yellow, orange brown, or gray with dark brown or black spots and blotches on its head, back, and legs. The upper body is almost completely covered with small, rounded warts. The frog has short but not thin front legs and longer hind legs. On the toes of each back foot, it has a black bump that it uses as a shovel, or spade, for digging. This bump, which is called a tubercle (TOO-ber-kul), gives the frog another common name, the mallee spadefoot. (A mallee is a shrubby area where a type of eucalyptus grows.) The painted frog has a short head with a rounded snout and two large eyes with vertical pupils. Males and females look similar except during the breeding season, when the males develop tiny spines on top of their warts, giving them a prickly look. Adults grow to 1.8 to 2.3 inches (4.6 to 5.8 centimeters) long from snout to rump.

Geographic range: Painted frogs live in south-central Australia, including South Australia, and likely Victoria and New South Wales.

Habitat: The painted frog lives in an area that typically has a very dry season and a rainy season. During the dry season, it stays underground in open forests or shrubby areas. In the wet, breeding season, it is found in grassy marshes, small ponds, and various pools of water.

Diet: The painted frog probably eats insects and other invertebrates, but scientists have not studied them closely enough to say for sure.

Behavior and reproduction: At the beginning of the dry season, this frog digs down into the soil. Once in a suitable underground spot, the outer layer of its skin peels up from its body, but stays in one piece and attached to the frog's body to form a coat, or cocoon. Snuggled inside its cocoon with only its nose poking out, the frog enters a state of deep sleep, called estivation, which lasts until the rainy season begins in fall or winter. Once the ground becomes wet, the cocoon splits open, and the frog digs itself out of the ground. The frog apparently does all of its feeding during the rainy season. It also breeds at this time.

Males of this species, which some people call trilling frogs, float in the water and begin calling. The call is a two- or three-second purring or trilling sound. Males and females meet at marshes or other shallow pools, and the females lay clumps of up to 1,000 small eggs in plants at the edge of the water. The eggs hatch into tadpoles, which may grow to be as much as 3.5 inches (9 centimeters) long from snout to tail tip before they change into froglets.

Painted frogs and people: People rarely see this burrowing frog. Those who handle these frogs must wash their hands, because the frog's warts can ooze a gooey slime that is believed to make people sick if they get it in their mouths and swallow it.

Conservation status: The World Conservation Union (IUCN) does not consider this species to be at risk. Although it is not common, its numbers appear to be staying about the same. Some of the frogs live in protected areas, but others live in places that may be developed into farmland, which could hurt the frogs in the future. ■

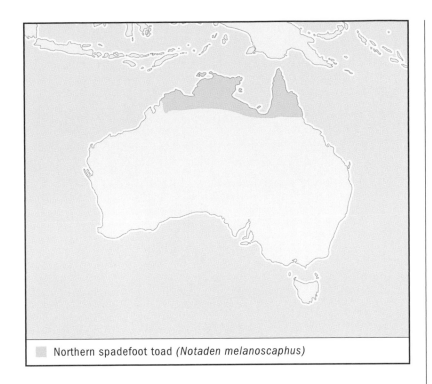

Northern spadefoot toad (Notaden melanoscaphus)

NORTHERN SPADEFOOT TOAD
Notaden melanoscaphus

Physical characteristics: Sitting as it often does with its short legs tucked against its body, the northern spadefoot toad has a shape like a golf ball. Some people even call this species a golfball frog. A small head with large eyes and a very short snout barely pokes out of its body. Its head, back, legs, and throat are brown to greenish brown or gray with black markings and are covered with warts. The warts may be tipped in white. Its belly is white. This frog has long, pointed toes and tubercles on its feet, similar to those of the painted frog, which give it the spadefoot name. Females usually grow to 1.8 to 1.9 inches (4.5 to 4.9 centimeters) long from snout to rump. The males sometimes are a bit smaller, usually reaching 1.3 to 1.9 inches (3.4 to 4.8 centimeters) in length.

Geographic range: The northern spadefoot toad lives in northern Australia, including parts of Kimberley, Western Australia, and Queensland.

Habitat: The northern spadefoot toad spends much of its life underground, but comes to the surface after heavy rains. It breeds in marshes, swamps, and small pools of water.

Diet: With the flip of a tongue out of the small mouth, the northern spadefoot frog snatches up small insects and other invertebrates to eat. The tadpoles appear to eat by straining tiny organisms out of the water.

Behavior and reproduction: This species uses the spades on its feet to burrow into the soil. In rainy weather, the northern spadefoot toad digs out of its underground home to look for insects, and in the breeding season, to mate. With its short legs and pudgy-looking body, this frog walks rather than hops and is not able to outrun most predators. It does, however, have a way of defending itself. When threatened, its warts ooze a gluey goop. A predator that unwisely bites at one of these frogs gets a mouth full of goop that quickly hardens, turns bright orange, and becomes difficult to clean off.

In the rainy, breeding season, males move to marshes, swamps, and newly filled pools of water and call from shallow spots. Their call is a loud, repeated "whoop." When the male calls, his body fills with air like a balloon. If he feels threatened, he will let the air out and sink out of sight. Males mate with females by climbing onto their backs and hanging on in front of the females' hind legs. Each female lays 500 to 1,400 eggs on the water's surface, and the eggs later sink and tangle in underwater plants as they hatch into tadpoles. The tadpoles turn into froglets when they are about two months old. The young froglets look much like the adults, but are often speckled with bright yellow, red, and black spots.

Northern spadefoot toads and people: People rarely see this frog.

Conservation status: The World Conservation Union (IUCN) does not consider this common species to be at risk. Some of its populations live in protected areas. ■

FOR MORE INFORMATION

Books:

Anstis, M. *Tadpoles of South-eastern Australia: A Guide with Keys.* Sydney: Reed New Holland, 2002.

Barker, John, Gordon C. Grigg, and Michael J. Tyler. *A Field Guide to Australian Frogs.* Chipping Norton, Australia: Surrey Beatty, 1995.

Campbell, A., ed. *Declines and Disappearances of Australian Frogs.* Canberra, Australia: Environment Australia, 1999.

Cogger, H. G. *Reptiles and Amphibians of Australia.* 6th edition. Sydney: Reed New Holland, 2001.

Cogger, H. G., E. E. Cameron, and H. M. Cogger. *Zoological Catalogue of Australia.* Vol. 1, *Amphibia and Reptilia.* Canberra, Australia: Australian Government Publishing Service, 1983.

Cronin, Leonard. *Key Guide to the Reptiles and Amphibians of Australia.* Sydney: Envirobooks, 2001.

Littlejohn, M. J., M. Davies, J. D. Roberts, and G. F. Watson. "Family Myobatrachidae." In *Fauna of Australia.* Vol. 2A, *Amphibia and Reptilia,* edited by C. J. Glasby, G. J. B. Ross, and P. Beesley. Canberra, Australia: AGPS, 1993.

Malone, B. S. "Mortality during the Early Life History Stages of the Baw Baw Frog, *Philoria frosti* (Anura: Myobatrachidae)." In *Biology of Australasian Frogs and Reptiles,* edited by G. Grigg, R. Shine, and H. Ehmann. Chipping Norton, Australia: Surrey Beatty and Sons, 1985.

Robinson, Martyn. *Field Guide to the Frogs of Australia.* Sydney: Reed New Holland, 1993.

Swan, Gerry. *Green Guide to Frogs of Australia.* Sydney: New Holland, 2001.

Web sites:

"Frogs—Amphibia." *Wildlife of Sydney.* http://faunanet.gov.au/wos/group.cfm?Group_ID=36 (accessed on February 24, 2005).

"Frogs of Australia." *Amphibian Research Centre.* http://frogs.org.au/frogs/index.html (accessed on February 24, 2005).

"Frogs of North Queensland." *James Cook University School of Tropical Biology.* http://www.jcu.edu.au/school/tbiol/zoology/herp/NthQldHerps/NthQLDHerps-frogs.shtml (accessed on February 24, 2005).

"The Frogs of NSW Wetlands - Other Frogs." *NSW Department of Land and Water Conservation.* http://www.dlwc.nsw.gov.au/care/wetlands/facts/paa/frogs/other_frogs.html (accessed on February 24, 2005).

"Information on Protecting Australian Frogs." *ASX Frog Focus.* http://www.asxfrogfocus.com/ (accessed on March 1, 2005).

"Useful Links and Frog Resources." *NSW National Parks and Wildlife Service.* http://www.nationalparks.nsw.gov.au/npws.nsf/Content/Useful+links+and+frog+resources (accessed on February 24, 2005).

AUSTRALIAN TOADLETS AND WATER FROGS
Myobatrachidae

Class: Amphibia

Order: Anura

Family: Myobatrachidae

Number of species: 121 species

phylum

class

subclass

order

monotypic order

suborder

▲ **family**

family
CHAPTER

PHYSICAL CHARACTERISTICS

Most of the Australian toadlets and water frogs are either small, slender creatures with long hind legs or tiny toads with short hind legs. Those members of the family that burrow head first, like the turtle frog, usually have powerful front legs and snouts that are tough, like the callous on a person's hand, while those that burrow hind end first, such as the northern toadlet, typically have hard bumps, called tubercles (TOO-ber-kulz), on their back feet to help them dig.

Overall, the Australian toadlets and water frogs range from 0.6 to 3.1 inches (1.6 to 7.9 centimeters) long from snout to rump, but the majority are on the smaller side. Typically, the frogs in this family are gray or brown, but often have brighter colored patches of skin that appear when they lift their front or back legs. Some, however, have bold colors all over their bodies. The Corroboree frog, for instance, is black and vivid yellow or green, while the sunset frog is covered in orange, red, and blue.

GEOGRAPHIC RANGE

Most of the species in this family live only in Australia, but at least two also are found in southern New Guinea.

HABITAT

Depending on the species, a frog in this family may live in a rainforest stream, a mountain meadow, a forest, a grassland that is dry much of the year, or in desert-like sand dunes near oceans. Many of them burrow into the soil or disappear under moss, leaf piles, or logs during the daytime. Even the tadpoles live in many habitats. Eggs and tadpoles may develop in a stream that flows all year, in a pond that will dry up later in the year, in a nest on land, or under the ground. In a few species, the eggs and/or tadpoles actually develop into frogs inside pockets on their fathers' hips, or inside their mothers' stomachs.

DIET

The Australian toadlets and water frogs eat arthropods (AR-thro-pawds), which are insects, spiders, and other invertebrates that have jointed legs. An invertebrate (in-VER-teh-breht) is an animal that does not have a backbone. Some species eat mainly one type of arthropod. The sandhill frog, for instance, eats mostly ants, even sometimes poking its head inside ant hills. In many cases, however, scientists do not know exactly which types of arthropods these species eat because they have not yet done thorough studies of the frogs.

BEHAVIOR AND REPRODUCTION

Most of the frogs in this family hide themselves away during the day. Some stay under damp leaves, moss, logs, or rocks on the ground, and others burrow. Burrowers may use their front legs to dig head first, or they may use their hind legs to scramble into the ground back end first. The turtle frog, which has a body with the shape of a turtle but without the shell, is a head-first burrower. It uses its short, but thick and strong front legs to scrape aside the sand and pushes its hard snout forward. A few species, such as Eungella torrent frog, may be active day or night. Some species that stay above ground for much of the year will burrow during the dry season and only return to the surface after the rainy weather returns.

In the breeding season, the males of some species set up and defend territories. For instance, male stonemason toadlets will get into wrestling matches over a good calling place. In other species, such as the quacking froglet, the males do not set up territories and instead chase after females. As many as five males may try to mate with a single female at the same time.

Most of the frogs in this family mate only at certain times of the year. For those that live in areas with dry and rainy seasons, the mating period usually happens in the rainy time of year. Usually, the males call only or mainly during the breeding season, although the males of some species call almost year-round.

Different species have different calls. For instance, the smooth toadlet makes a buzzy, creaking sound, the eastern sign-bearing froglet gives a loud "eeek," and the Victorian smooth froglet has a repeating call that starts with a short quacking noise and follows with a repeated "tik-tik-tik-tik-tik-tik-tik." Most males call only at night, but those species that are active during the day also call sometimes in broad daylight. The moss frog, for example, makes its knocking call in the daytime from a hiding spot among plants on the floor of its mountain rainforests. Depending on the species, the males may call from underground, from a stream, pond or other watering hole, or from a hiding place on land, as the moss frog does.

Usually, the males and females pair and mate at the calling site. To mate, the male must climb onto the female's back as she lays her eggs. In a few species, however, the male calls not from the watering hole where he will mate, but from land a distance away. When a female approaches him, he climbs onto her back and she carries him to the water. The floodplain toadlet does things a little differently. Instead of the male climbing onto the female's back, she squirms underneath him while he is calling. Once she is fully beneath him, he stops calling, holds onto her, and they move to the water to mate.

The females of some of the species in this family, like the tinkling frog, mate in the water and lay their eggs there. Their eggs hatch into tadpoles that swim off in the water and eventually turn into froglets. Others, such as the red-backed toadlet, lay their eggs on land. When rains drench the land, the eggs hatch into tadpoles that float in the rainwater or squirm on the wet soil to get to a pond or other watering hole, where they eventually change into froglets. Moss frogs also lay their eggs on land, but their tadpoles survive without a pond or even a puddle. Moss frog eggs are large and coated with jelly. When the tadpoles are born, they live in

THAT'S A MOUTHFUL!

The female gastric brooding frog of Australia takes very good care of her young. After she lays up to two dozen eggs, she puts them in an especially safe place where they can develop and grow, and that place is inside her stomach. Normally, the stomach acids digest things that animals eat, but the acid in these frogs' bellies turns off so the eggs can safely turn into tadpoles and then froglets inside the female's stomach. When the froglets are finally born, they leave her body the same way they came in: through her mouth. Scientists had just begun studying these unusual animals for use in controlling stomach acid in humans when the frogs disappeared. One of the two gastric brooding frog species vanished in 1983, and the second species, which was just discovered in 1983, disappeared in 1985. The IUCN now considers both to be Extinct. The same method that the frog used to turn off its stomach acid is now used in medicines to help people who have stomach ulcers. An ulcer is a sore on the wall of the stomach.

TANGLED FAMILY LINES

Organizing the species of gastric brooding frogs, Australian toadlets and water frogs, and Australian ground frogs has been a confusing chore. Some people lump them all together into one family, while others separate them into three families. Scientists have been studying bones, fossils, and other characteristics to sort it out. For now, however, this book takes the middle ground with two families: the Limnodynastidae for the Australian ground frogs and the Myobatrachidae for the Australian toadlets and water frogs as well as the two recently extinct species of gastric brooding frogs.

the leftover jelly for more than a year, even surviving under a layer of winter snow. After about 13 months, they finally turn into froglets. Female sandhill frogs and a few other species lay their gel-covered eggs underground. These eggs hatch into froglets, skipping the tadpole stage.

Perhaps oddest of all are the hip pocket frogs and the gastric brooding frogs. Female hip pocket frogs lay their eggs in and/or under damp leaves on the ground. The female stays with her eggs until they are ready to hatch. The male then takes over. He rests the front part of his body on the hatching eggs, and up to a dozen newborn tadpoles squirm up the sides of his body and into his two pouches, one of which is on each hip. In about two months, froglets crawl out of the pockets to face the world. In the gastric brooding frogs, on the other hand, the female takes charge. After she lays her eggs, she swallows them. The eggs turn into tadpoles and then froglets in her stomach and leave her body through her mouth. While the eggs are in her stomach, she stops eating.

AUSTRALIAN TOADLETS, WATER FROGS, AND PEOPLE

For the most part, people do not see these mostly night-active frogs in the wild. They are also uncommon in the pet trade. Scientists are interested in the skin of many of these frogs, because it oozes a gooey fluid that may one day be useful in making medicines.

CONSERVATION STATUS

According to the World Conservation Union (IUCN), three species are Extinct and are no longer in existence, and six are Critically Endangered, which means that they face an extremely high risk of extinction in the wild. In addition, two are Endangered and face a very high risk of extinction in the wild; four are Vulnerable and face a high risk of extinction in the wild; and three are Near Threatened and at risk of becoming threatened with extinction in the future. The IUCN also lists six as Data Deficient, which means that there is not enough information to make a judgment about their threat of extinction.

The three extinct species are the northern gastric brooding frog, which is sometimes known as the Eungella gastric brooding frog; the southern gastric brooding frog, also called the Conondale or platypus gastric brooding frog; and the Mount Glorious day frog, which also goes by the names Mount Glorious torrent frog or southern day frog. The northern and southern gastric brooding frogs vanished in 1983–1985, and although the Mount Glorious day frog was quite common in the early 1970s, it disappeared in 1979. Scientists do not know what caused the three species to die out, but they suspect that changes to their habitats, including the loss of trees and native plants, and infection with a fungus may be at least partly to blame.

Scientists are also unsure why the numbers of many other at-risk species are dropping. The Corroboree frog, which is Critically Endangered, is an example. This small species lives in mountain grasslands and forests. It is a beautiful, shiny black frog, with bright yellow or green stripes. In just 10 years, the number of adults living in the wild dropped from about 2,000 to fewer than 250 in 2004. Some scientists believe that differences in the weather, fungus infections, or habitat changes may be playing a role in the disappearance of the frogs, but they do not know for sure.

Studies of other at-risk frogs, however, have revealed why they are vanishing. The white-bellied frog, which is Critically Endangered, has become less and less common. As of 2004, it only lived in a few areas of the southwestern edge of Western Australia. Scientists believe that this burrowing frog has suffered because of habitat loss. According to the IUCN, about 70 percent of the habitat where this frog might live and breed has been logged or otherwise cleared since humans arrived in this part of Australia. The frogs now live in small groups here and there where the habitat is still in good shape.

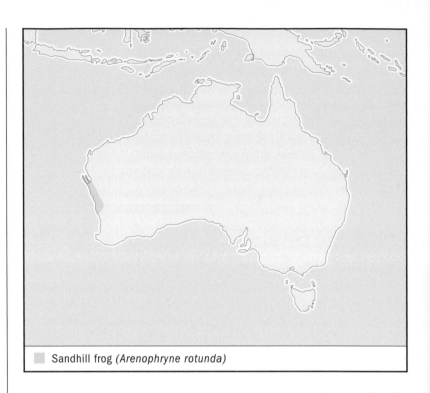

Sandhill frog (*Arenophryne rotunda*)

SANDHILL FROG
Arenophryne rotunda

Physical characteristics: The sandhill frog, which also goes by the name of round frog, is a chubby little creature with toad-like features. It has a round, somewhat flat body with small hind legs and short, but strong front legs. The first toe on each of the unusually wide front feet is very small. The tiny head has a short, rounded snout with a hard, callous-like tip. Sandhill frogs are usually very light gray with darker gray and sometimes rust-colored speckles on the warty head, back, and legs. They also have a narrow, light-colored, sometimes hard-to-see, stripe down the middle of the back. Males and females look alike. Females grow to 1.1 to 1.3 inches (2.8 to 3.3 centimeters) long from snout to rump, and males usually reach 1 to 1.3 inches (2.6 to 3.3 centimeters) in length.

Geographic range: Sandhill frogs live along the ocean in far western Australia from Kalbarri to Shark Bay and Dirk Hartog Island.

Habitat: Sandhill frogs live in desert-like sand dunes along the ocean's coast and stay underground during the day. At night, when the air is more humid, they look for food on land. Unlike most other frogs, this unusual species does not need any ponds, streams, or even puddles of water to survive. Instead, it gets most of its moisture from the damp sand underground.

Diet: Their diet includes ants, beetles, spiders, and other arthropods.

Behavior and reproduction: A sandhill frog digs head first into the sand, making good use of its hard snout and strong front legs. It stays underground during the day, digging deep enough to reach damp sand. At night, it crawls out of the sand and starts looking for food. It does not hop, instead walking across the dunes and leaving tiny, wide-spaced footprints behind. The males call from April to July, which is late fall in Australia, but do it underground. The males and females pair up, sometimes with several pairs in the same place, and the females lay their eggs from September to December, also underground and usually about 31.5 inches (80 centimeters) deep. The young skip the tadpole stage, and froglets hatch out of the eggs.

Unlike most other frogs, this unusual species does not need any ponds, streams, or even puddles of water to survive. Instead, it gets most of its moisture from the damp sand underground. (Kelvin Aitken/Peter Arnold, Inc.)

Sandhill frogs and people: Most people only see this animal's footprints, rarely the frog.

Conservation status: This frog is quite common in the sand dunes where it lives and is not considered to be at risk. ■

Hip pocket frog (*Assa darlingtoni*)

HIP POCKET FROG
Assa darlingtoni

Physical characteristics: Also called a pouched frog or marsupial frog, the hip pocket frog is best known for the pouch above each hind leg of the male. Each of his pouches is large enough to hold several eggs, but unless they are filled, the pockets are difficult to see and only visible as small slits. Hip pocket frogs have a rather wide body, which may be brown, pinkish brown, gray, or red. They commonly have a dark brown stripe that starts behind the eye, carries over the shoulder and onto the side of the frog behind its front leg. Their legs may have dark or faded brown bands, and all four feet end in pad-tipped toes. The underside of the frog is white. Females usually grow to 0.7 to 0.8 inches (18 to 21 centimeters) long, and males are usually about 0.1 inches shorter.

Geographic range: Hip pocket frogs live in mountains along the border of New South Wales and Queensland and in northeastern Australia.

Habitat: Hip pocket frogs make their home in the mountain rainforests that are thick with trees and plants. They usually stay out of

Hip pocket frogs make their home in the mountain rainforests that are thick with trees and plants. (Illustration by Barbara Duperron. Reproduced by permission.)

view in deep piles of leaves, under rocks, or in other hiding places on the forest floor.

Diet: They eat various arthropods.

Behavior and reproduction: Scientists know little about their behavior outside of breeding and reproduction. The breeding season begins when the males start to make their calls, which are fast, repeated, buzzy sounds. The females follow the calls to the male's hiding spot under a log or in the leaves on the ground. When a female gets closer, the male calls even more. The male climbs onto her back and mates with her as she lays her eggs, which fall onto the damp dirt and rotting leaves. The female stays with her eggs for several days until they are ready to hatch. The male then moves in and covers the hatching eggs with the front part of his body. Tadpoles wiggle out of the eggs, up his sides, and into his hip pouches. A single male can have as many as six tadpoles in each of his two pockets. The tadpoles stay inside. Each has yolk left over from its egg that it can eat and so does not need to find any other food. In 48 to 69 days, the tadpoles change into froglets and crawl out of the male's pockets to live life on their own.

Hip pocket frogs and people: People rarely see this small frog.

Conservation status: The hip pocket frog is not considered endangered or threatened. ■

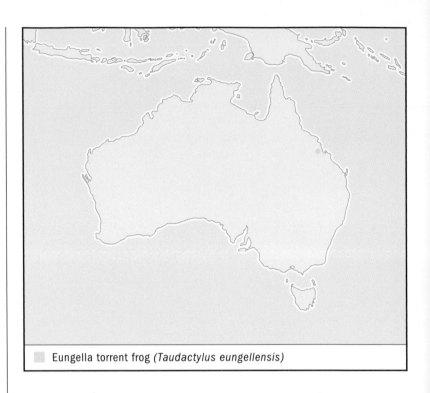
Eungella torrent frog *(Taudactylus eungellensis)*

EUNGELLA TORRENT FROG
Taudactylus eungellensis

Physical characteristics: Also known as the Eungella day frog, the Eungella torrent frog is a light brown or gray frog with dark brown markings on its head, back, and legs. The markings on its head include one wide blotch that stretches between its two large eyes. The markings on its hind legs may look like bands. Its body is rather long and thin, and it also has slender front and hind legs. The toes on each of its four feet widen out at the end into pads, and the bones inside the tips of the toes are T-shaped. The hind legs are much longer that the front pair. Its throat and belly are creamy white with a touch of yellow on the thighs and lower belly. Some have smooth backs, but others have scattered, small bumps. Males and females look similar, but the males are usually a bit smaller. Males grow to 1 to 1.1 inches (2.5 to 2.8 centimeters) long from the tip of the snout to the end of the rump, while females normally reach 1.1 to 1.4 inches (2.8 to 3.6 centimeters) in length.

This was a common species until 1985, when scientists began noticing that the torrent frogs were quickly disappearing. In the late 1980s, they feared the frogs might be extinct, but the frogs turned up again in 1992. (Illustration by Barbara Duperron. Reproduced by permission.)

Geographic range: Eungella torrent frogs live in a small mountainous area of mid-eastern Queensland, Australia.

Habitat: The frogs spend their days in small or large, swift mountain streams located at 490 to 3,280 feet (150 to 1,000 meters) above sea level or in the thick plants of the surrounding rainforest.

Diet: Scientists are unsure, but they think Eungella torrent frogs eat different types of arthropods.

Behavior and reproduction: Eungella torrent frogs may be active day and night, often sitting on or under rocks along the river or near waterfalls where they can feel the splash of the crashing water. They often bob their heads or wave their hind legs, apparently a way to communicate. The males may call year-round, although they tend to do more calling and mating from January to May, which is the summer and fall in Australia. The call is a soft rattle. The females lay 30 to 50 eggs at a time, and these hatch into tadpoles. The tadpoles, which have suction cups around their mouths, usually move about at the bottom of the stream until they change into froglets in November, December, and January.

Eungella torrent frogs and people: Very few people have seen this rare frog.

Conservation status: According to the World Conservation Union (IUCN), this species is Critically Endangered, which means that it faces an extremely high risk of extinction in the wild. This was a common species until 1985, when scientists began noticing that the torrent frogs were quickly disappearing. In the late 1980s, they feared the frogs might be extinct, but the frogs turned up again in 1992. They now live in nine spots inside Eungella National Park, and their numbers seem to be climbing very slowly. Scientists do not know what caused the frogs to decline in the 1980s and are watching this species closely. ■

FOR MORE INFORMATION

Books:

Anstis, M. *Tadpoles of South-eastern Australia: A Guide with Keys.* Sydney: Reed New Holland, 2002.

Barker, John, Gordon C. Grigg, and Michael J. Tyler. *A Field Guide to Australian Frogs.* Chipping Norton, Australia: Surrey Beatty, 1995.

Campbell, A., ed. *Declines and Disappearances of Australian Frogs.* Canberra, Australia: Environment Australia, 1999.

Cogger, H. G. *Reptiles and Amphibians of Australia.* 6th edition. Sydney: Reed New Holland, 2001.

Cogger, Harold G., and Richard G. Zweifel. *Encyclopedia of Reptiles and Amphibians.* San Diego, CA: Academic Press, 1998.

Cogger, H. G., E. E. Cameron, and H. M. Cogger. *Zoological Catalogue of Australia.* Vol. 1, *Amphibia and Reptilia.* Canberra, Australia: Australian Government Publishing Service, 1983.

Cronin, Leonard. *Key Guide to the Reptiles and Amphibians of Australia.* Sydney: Envirobooks, 2001.

Ehmann, H., and G. Swan. "Reproduction and Development in the Marsupial Frog *Assa darlingtoni* (Leptodactylidae: Anura)." In *Biology of Australasian Frogs and Reptiles,* edited by G. Grigg, R. Shine, and H. Ehmann. Chipping Norton, Australia: Surrey Beatty and Sons, 1985.

Halliday, Tim, and Kraig Adler, eds. *The Encyclopedia of Reptiles and Amphibians (Smithsonian Handbooks).* New York: Facts on File, 1991.

Littlejohn, M. J., M. Davies, J. D. Roberts, and G. F. Watson. "Family Myobatrachidae." In *Fauna of Australia.* Vol. 2A, *Amphibia and Reptilia,* edited by C. J. Glasby, G. J. B. Ross, and P. Beesley. Canberra, Australia: AGPS, 1993.

Miller, Sara Swan. *Frogs and Toads: The Leggy Leapers.* New York: Franklin Watts, 2000.

Roberts, J. D. "The Biology of *Arenophryne rotunda* (Anura: Myobatrachidae): A Burrowing Frog from Shark Bay, Western Australia."

In *Research in Shark Bay, Report of the France-Australe Bicentennary Expedition Committee,* edited by P. F. Berry, S. D. Bradshaw, and B. R. Wilson. Perth, Australia: West Australian Museum, 1990.

Robinson, Martyn. *Field Guide to the Frogs of Australia.* Sydney: Reed New Holland, 1993.

Swan, Gerry. *Green Guide to Frogs of Australia.* Sydney: New Holland, 2001.

Tyler, Michael J. *Australian Frogs: A Natural History.* Ithaca, NY: Cornell University Press, 1994.

Tyler, M. J., ed. *The Gastric Brooding Frog.* London and Canberra: Croom Helm, 1983.

Periodicals:

Sunquist, Fiona. "Really Weird, Really Wild!" *National Geographic World* (February 1999): 3.

Web sites:

"Corroboree Frog." *Kidcyber.* http://www.kidcyber.com.au/topics/frog_corrob.htm (accessed on March 1, 2005).

"Frogs — Amphibia." *Wildlife of Sydney.* http://faunanet.gov.au/wos/group.cfm?Group_ID=36 (accessed on February 24, 2005).

"Frogs of Australia." *Amphibian Research Centre.* http://frogs.org.au/frogs/index.html (accessed on February 24, 2005).

"The Frogs of NSW Wetlands - Other Frogs." *NSW Department of Land and Water Conservation.* http://www.dlwc.nsw.gov.au/care/wetlands/facts/paa/frogs/other_frogs.html (accessed on February 24, 2005).

"Information on Protecting Australian Frogs." *ASX Frog Focus.* http://www.asxfrogfocus.com/ (accessed on March 1, 2005).

Jamal, Rina Abdul. "Marsupial (Pouched) Frog." *AnimalFact.com.* http://www.animalfact.com/article1020.htm (accessed on March 2, 2005).

"Useful Links and Frog Resources." *NSW National Parks and Wildlife Service.* http://www.nationalparks.nsw.gov.au/npws.nsf/Content/Useful+links+and+frog+resources (accessed on February 24, 2005).

Species List by Biome

CONIFEROUS FOREST
Ailao moustache toad
Annam broad-headed toad
Bana leaf litter frog
Brown frog
Cascade torrent salamander
Coastal giant salamander
Eastern narrow-mouthed toad
European fire salamander
Fire-bellied toad
Great crested newt
Mandarin salamander
Oriental fire-bellied toad
Schmidt's lazy toad
Smooth newt
Two-lined salamander
Yellow-bellied toad

DECIDUOUS FOREST
Arboreal salamander
Asian horned frog
Bell's salamander
Brown frog
Cascade torrent salamander
Common squeaker
Darwin's frog
Eastern narrow-mouthed toad
European fire salamander
Fire-bellied toad

Golden-striped salamander
Goliath frog
Great crested newt
Green treefrog
Hairy frog
Hamilton's frog
Harlequin frog
Kinugasa flying frog
Lynch's Cochran frog
Mandarin salamander
Marine toad
Maud Island frog
Mesoamerican burrowing toad
Mexican caecilian
Micro frog
Mocquard's rain frog
Natal ghost frog
Nilgiri tropical frog
Oriental fire-bellied toad
Pacific giant glass frog
Painted frog
Painted Indonesian treefrog
Painted reed frog
Paradox frog
Parsley frog
Phantasmal poison frog
Pumpkin toadlet
Rock River frog
Rocky Mountain tailed frog
Ruthven's frog

South American bullfrog
Smooth newt
Sumaco horned treefrog
Talamancan web-footed
  salamander
Tusked frog
Two-lined salamander
Yellow-bellied toad
Yucatecan shovel-headed
  treefrog

DESERT
Sandhill frog
Water-holding frog

GRASSLAND
Asian horned frog
Banded rubber frog
Brown frog
Bubbling kassina
Budgett's frog
Darwin's frog
Fire-bellied toad
Gray four-eyed frog
Great crested newt
Mandarin salamander
Marbled snout-burrower
Marine toad
Mesoamerican burrowing toad

Mocquard's rain frog
Natal ghost frog
Northern spadefoot toad
Oriental fire-bellied toad
Painted frog
Painted reed frog
Paradox frog
Parsley frog
Patagonia frog
Plains spadefoot toad
Pointed-tongue floating frog
Riobamba marsupial frog
Smooth newt
Tiger salamander
Tusked frog
Yellow-bellied toad
Yucatecan shovel-headed
  treefrog
Water-holding frog

LAKE AND POND
Amazonian skittering frog
Brown frog
Bubbling kassina
Bullfrog
Common plantanna (African
  clawed frog)
Eastern narrow-mouthed toad
Fire-bellied toad
Golden-striped salamander
Gray four-eyed frog
Great crested newt
Hokkaido salamander
Hourglass treefrog
Japanese fire-bellied newt
Lesser siren
Mandarin salamander
Marine toad
Midwife toad
Mudpuppy
Olm
Oriental fire-bellied toad
Painted frog
Painted reed frog
Paradox frog
Patagonia frog

Perez's snouted frog
Phantasmal poison frog
Philippine barbourula
Pointed-tongue floating frog
Pyburn's pancake frog
Riobamba marsupial frog
Smooth newt
South American bullfrog
Surinam horned frog
Surinam toad
Three-toed amphiuma
Tropical clawed frog
Two-lined salamander
Yellow-bellied toad

RAINFOREST
African wart frog
Amazonian skittering frog
Blue-toed rocket frog
Eungella torrent frog
Free Madagascar frog
Golden dart-poison frog
Golden toad
Gold-striped frog
Hip pocket frog
Hourglass treefrog
Kirk's caecilian
La Palma glass frog
Long-fingered slender toad
Marbled caecilian
Perez's snouted frog
Philippine barbourula
Pyburn's pancake frog
Red caecilian
Ruthven's frog
Seychelles frog
South American bullfrog
Surinam horned frog
Tusked frog
Wilhelm rainforest frog

RIVER AND STREAM
Ailao moustache toad
Annam broad-headed toad
Asian horned frog

Brown frog
Bullfrog
Cascade torrent salamander
Cayenne caecilian
Ceylon caecilian
Coastal giant salamander
Common plantanna (African
  clawed frog)
Darwin's frog
Dusky salamander
Eungella torrent frog
Fire-bellied toad
Goliath frog
Green treefrog
Hairy frog
Harlequin frog
Hellbender
Hokkaido salamander
Japanese clawed salamander
La Palma glass frog
Lesser siren
Long-fingered slender toad
Lynch's Cochran frog
Marbled caecilian
Midwife toad
Mudpuppy
Natal ghost frog
Nilgiri tropical frog
Olm
Oriental fire-bellied toad
Pacific giant glass frog
Painted frog
Painted reed frog
Paradox frog
Phantasmal poison frog
Philippine barbourula
Pyburn's pancake frog
Rock River frog
Rocky Mountain tailed frog
Ruthven's frog
Schmidt's lazy toad
Semirechensk salamander
South American bullfrog
Surinam toad
Texas blind salamander
Three-toed amphiuma

Tropical clawed frog
Two-lined salamander
Yellow-bellied toad

WETLAND
Banded rubber frog
Bubbling kassina
Budgett's frog
Brown frog
Bullfrog
Ceylon caecilian
Common plantanna (African
  clawed frog)
Darwin's frog

Eastern narrow-mouthed toad
Fire-bellied toad
Free Madagascar frog
Green treefrog
Kinugasa flying frog
Kirk's caecilian
Lesser siren
Malaysian painted frog
Marbled snout-burrower
Marine toad
Micro frog
Mocquard's rain frog
Northern spadefoot toad
Oriental fire-bellied toad
Painted frog

Painted reed frog
Paradox frog
Perez's snouted frog
Pointed-tongue floating frog
Riobamba marsupial frog
Ruthven's frog
Schmidt's lazy toad
Semirechensk salamander
Surinam horned frog
Surinam toad
Three-toed amphiuma
Yellow-bellied toad
Yucatecan shovel-headed
  treefrog
Water-holding frog

Species List by Geographic Range

ALBANIA
Brown frog
European fire salamander
Great crested newt
Smooth newt

ALGERIA
Painted frog

ANDORRA
European fire salamander
Great crested newt
Smooth newt

ANGOLA
Bubbling kassina
Common plantanna (African
  clawed frog)
Hairy frog
Marbled snout-burrower
Painted reed frog
Tropical clawed frog

ARGENTINA
Budgett's frog
Darwin's frog
Gray four-eyed frog
Marine toad

Patagonia frog

ARMENIA
Brown frog

AUSTRALIA
Eungella torrent frog
Green treefrog
Hip pocket frog
Marine toad
Northern spadefoot toad
Painted frog
Sandhill frog
Tusked frog
Water-holding frog

AUSTRIA
Brown frog
European fire salamander
Fire-bellied toad
Great crested newt
Smooth newt
Yellow-bellied toad

BAHAMAS
Eastern narrow-mouthed toad

BELARUS
European fire salamander
Great crested newt
Smooth newt

BELGIUM
Brown frog
European fire salamander
Great crested newt
Midwife toad
Parsley frog
Smooth newt

BELIZE
Marine toad
Mesoamerican burrowing toad
Mexican caecilian
Yucatecan shovel-headed
  treefrog

BENIN
Bubbling Kassina
Goliath frog
Painted reed frog

BOLIVIA
Amazonian skittering frog
Budgett's frog

Hourglass treefrog
Marine toad
Perez's snouted frog
Surinam toad

BOSNIA AND HERZEGOVINA
European fire salamander
Great crested newt
Olm
Smooth newt

BOTSWANA
Bubbling kassina
Common plantanna (African clawed frog)
Painted reed frog

BRAZIL
Amazonian skittering frog
Blue-toed rocket frog
Cayenne caecilian
Gold-striped frog
Hourglass treefrog
Marine toad
Paradox frog
Perez's snouted frog
Pumpkin toadlet
Rock River frog
Ruthven's frog
South American bullfrog
Surinam horned frog
Surinam toad

BULGARIA
European fire salamander
Great crested newt
Smooth newt

BURKINA FASO
Bubbling kassina
Painted reed frog

BURUNDI
Bubbling kassina
Common plantanna (African clawed frog)
Painted reed frog

CAMBODIA
Pointed-tongue floating frog

CAMEROON
African wart frog
Bubbling kassina
Common plantanna (African clawed frog)
Goliath frog
Hairy frog
Marbled snout-burrower
Painted reed frog
Tropical clawed frog

CANADA
Bullfrog
Coastal giant salamander
Coastal tailed frog
Dusky salamander
Mudpuppy
Plains spadefoot toad
Rocky Mountain tailed frog
Tiger salamander
Two-lined salamander

CHAD
Bubbling kassina
Painted reed frog

CHILE
Common plantanna (African clawed frog)
Darwin's frog
Gray four-eyed frog
Marine toad

CHINA
Ailao moustache toad

Malaysian painted frog
Mandarin salamander
Oriental fire-bellied toad
Pointed-tongue floating frog
Schmidt's lazy toad
Semirechensk salamander

COLOMBIA
Amazonian skittering frog
Cayenne caecilian
Golden dart-poison frog
Gold-striped frog
Hourglass treefrog
La Palma glass frog
Lynch's Cochran frog
Marine toad
Pacific giant glass frog
Perez's snouted frog
Pyburn's pancake frog
South American bullfrog
Sumaco horned treefrog
Surinam horned frog
Surinam toad

COSTA RICA
Golden toad
Harlequin frog
La Palma glass frog
Marine toad
Mesoamerican burrowing toad
Mexican caecilian
South American bullfrog
Talamancan web-footed salamander

CROATIA
European fire salamander
Great crested newt
Olm
Smooth newt

CYPRUS
Brown frog

CZECH REPUBLIC
Brown frog
European fire salamander
Great crested newt
Smooth newt

DEMOCRATIC REPUBLIC OF THE CONGO
Common plantanna (African
  clawed frog)
Common squeaker
Hairy frog
Marbled snout-burrower

DENMARK
Brown frog
European fire salamander
Fire-bellied toad
Great crested newt
Smooth newt

ECUADOR
Hourglass treefrog
La Palma glass frog
Marbled caecilian
Marine toad
Pacific giant glass frog
Phantasmal poison frog
Riobamba marsupial frog
South American bullfrog
Sumaco horned treefrog
Surinam toad

EL SALVADOR
Marine toad
Mesoamerican burrowing toad
Mexican caecilian

EQUATORIAL GUINEA
Common plantanna (African
  clawed frog)
Hairy frog

Marbled snout-burrower

ESTONIA
Brown frog
European fire salamander
Great crested newt
Smooth newt

ETHIOPIA
Bubbling kassina
Ethiopian snout-burrower
  (Lake Zwai snout-burrower)
Painted reed frog

FINLAND
Brown frog
European fire salamander
Great crested newt
Smooth newt

FRANCE
Brown frog
European fire salamander
Great crested newt
Midwife toad
Painted frog
Parsley frog
Smooth newt

FRENCH GUIANA
Cayenne caecilian
Gold-striped frog
Hourglass treefrog
Marine toad
Paradox frog
Pyburn's pancake frog
Ruthven's frog
South American bullfrog
Surinam toad
Surinam horned frog

GABON
African wart frog

Bubbling kassina
Common plantanna (African
  clawed frog)
Hairy frog
Marbled snout-burrower
Painted reed frog
Tropical clawed frog

GERMANY
Brown frog
Common plantanna (African
  clawed frog)
European fire salamander
Fire-bellied toad
Great crested newt
Midwife toad
Smooth newt

GHANA
Bubbling kassina
Goliath frog
Painted reed frog

GREECE
Brown frog
European fire salamander
Fire-bellied toad
Great crested newt
Smooth newt
Yellow-bellied toad

GUATEMALA
Marine toad
Mesoamerican burrowing toad
Mexican caecilian
Yucatecan shovel-headed
  treefrog

GUINEA
Bubbling kassina
Goliath frog
Painted reed frog

GUINEA-BISSAU
Bubbling kassina
Painted reed frog

GUYANA
Cayenne caecilian
Gold-striped frog
Hourglass treefrog
Marine toad
Paradox frog
Pyburn's pancake frog
Ruthven's frog
South American bullfrog
Surinam horned frog
Surinam toad

HONDURAS
Marine toad
Mesoamerican burrowing toad
Mexican caecilian
South American bullfrog
Yucatecan shovel-headed
  treefrog

HUNGARY
Brown frog
European fire salamander
Great crested newt
Smooth newt
Yellow-bellied toad

INDIA
Mandarin salamander
Nilgiri tropical frog
Pointed-tongue floating frog
Red caecilian

INDONESIA
Asian horned frog
Long-fingered slender toad
Malaysian painted frog
Painted Indonesian treefrog
Pointed-tongue floating frog

IRELAND
European fire salamander
Great crested newt
Smooth newt

ITALY
Brown frog
European fire salamander
Great crested newt
Olm
Painted frog
Parsley frog
Smooth newt
Yellow-bellied toad

IVORY COAST
Bubbling kassina
Goliath frog
Painted reed frog

JAPAN
Hokkaido salamander
Japanese clawed salamander
Japanese fire-bellied newt
Kinugasa flying frog
Marine toad
Oriental fire-bellied toad

KAZAKHSTAN
Semirechensk salamander

KENYA
Banded rubber frog
Bubbling kassina
Common plantanna (African
  clawed frog)
Common squeaker
Marbled snout-burrower
Painted reed frog

KOREA
(NORTH AND SOUTH)
Oriental fire-bellied toad

LAOS
Bana leaf litter frog

LATVIA
European fire salamander
Great crested newt
Smooth newt

LESOTHO
Bubbling kassina
Common plantanna (African
  clawed frog)
Natal ghost frog
Painted reed frog
Tropical clawed frog

LIBERIA
Bubbling kassina
Goliath frog
Painted reed frog

LIECHTENSTEIN
European fire salamander
Great crested newt
Smooth newt

LITHUANIA
European fire salamander
Great crested newt
Smooth newt

LUXEMBOURG
Brown frog
European fire salamander
Great crested newt
Midwife toad
Parsley frog
Smooth newt

MACEDONIA
European fire salamander
Great crested newt
Smooth newt

MADAGASCAR
Free Madagascar frog
Mocquard's rain frog

MALAWI
Bubbling kassina
Common plantanna (African clawed frog)
Kirk's caecilian
Painted reed frog

MALAYSIA
Asian horned frog
Malaysian painted frog
Painted Indonesian treefrog
Pointed-tongue floating frog

MALI
Bubbling kassina
Painted reed frog

MALTA
Brown frog
European fire salamander
Great crested newt
Painted frog
Smooth newt

MEXICO
Arboreal salamander
Bell's salamander
Bullfrog
Lesser siren
Marine toad
Mesoamerican burrowing toad
Mexican caecilian
Plains spadefoot toad
Tiger salamander
Yucatecan shovel-headed treefrog

MOLDOVA
European fire salamander

Great crested newt
Smooth newt

MONACO
European fire salamander
Great crested newt
Smooth newt

MOROCCO
Painted frog

MOZAMBIQUE
Banded rubber frog
Bubbling kassina
Common plantanna (African clawed frog)
Common squeaker
Marbled snout-burrower
Painted reed frog

NAMIBIA
Bubbling kassina
Common plantanna (African clawed frog)
Painted reed frog
Tropical clawed frog

NEPAL
Mandarin salamander

NETHERLANDS
Brown frog
European fire salamander
Great crested newt
Midwife toad
Smooth newt

NEW ZEALAND
Green treefrog
Hamilton's frog
Maud Island frog

NICARAGUA
Marine toad
Mesoamerican burrowing toad
Mexican caecilian
South American bullfrog

NIGER
Bubbling kassina
Painted reed frog

NIGERIA
Bubbling kassina
Goliath frog
Hairy frog
Marbled snout-burrower
Painted reed frog

NORWAY
Brown frog
European fire salamander
Great crested newt
Smooth newt

PANAMA
Harlequin frog
La Palma glass frog
Marine toad
Mexican caecilian
South American bullfrog

PAPUA NEW GUINEA
Wilhelm rainforest frog

PARAGUAY
Budgett's frog
Marine toad

PERU
Amazonian skittering frog
Cayenne caecilian
Gold-striped frog
Hourglass treefrog

Marine toad
Perez's snouted frog
Phantasmal poison frog
Ruthven's frog
South American bullfrog
Sumaco horned treefrog
Surinam toad
Surinam horned frog

PHILIPPINES
Asian horned frog
Marine toad
Painted Indonesian treefrog
Philippine barbourula

POLAND
European fire salamander
Fire-bellied toad
Great crested newt
Smooth newt

PORTUGAL
Brown frog
European fire salamander
Golden-striped salamander
Great crested newt
Midwife toad
Parsley frog
Smooth newt

REPUBLIC OF THE CONGO
African wart frog
Common plantanna (African clawed frog)
Tropical clawed frog

ROMANIA
European fire salamander
Great crested newt
Smooth newt

RUSSIA

European fire salamander
Great crested newt
Oriental fire-bellied toad
Smooth newt

RWANDA
Bubbling kassina
Common plantanna (African clawed frog)
Painted reed frog

SAN MARINO
European fire salamander
Great crested newt
Smooth newt

SÃO TOMÉ AND PRÍNCIPE
Common plantanna (African clawed frog)

SENEGAL
Bubbling kassina
Painted reed frog

SERBIA-MONTENEGRO
European fire salamander
Great crested newt
Olm
Smooth newt

SEYCHELLES
Seychelles frog

SIERRA LEONE
Bubbling kassina
Goliath frog
Painted reed frog

SINGAPORE
Painted Indonesian treefrog

SLOVAKIA
European fire salamander
Great crested newt
Smooth newt

SLOVENIA
European fire salamander
Great crested newt
Olm
Smooth newt

SOMALIA
Banded rubber frog

SOUTH AFRICA
Banded rubber frog
Bubbling kassina
Common plantanna (African clawed frog)
Common squeaker
Marbled snout-burrower
Micro frog
Natal ghost frog
Painted reed frog
Tropical clawed frog

SPAIN
Brown frog
European fire salamander
Golden-striped salamander
Great crested newt
Midwife toad
Painted frog
Parsley frog
Smooth newt

SRI LANKA
Ceylon caecilian

SUDAN
Bubbling kassina
Painted reed frog

SURINAME
Cayenne caecilian
Gold-striped frog
Hourglass treefrog
Marine toad
Paradox frog
Pyburn's pancake frog
Ruthven's frog
South American bullfrog
Surinam horned frog
Surinam toad

SWAZILAND
Bubbling kassina
Common plantanna (African
  clawed frog)
Natal ghost frog
Painted reed frog

SWEDEN
Brown frog
European fire salamander
Fire-bellied toad
Great crested newt
Smooth newt

SWITZERLAND
Brown frog
European fire salamander
Great crested newt
Midwife toad
Smooth newt
Yellow-bellied toad

TAIWAN
Malaysian painted frog
Painted Indonesian treefrog

TANZANIA
Banded rubber frog
Bubbling kassina
Common plantanna (African
  clawed frog)
Kirk's caecilian

Painted reed frog

THAILAND
Asian horned frog
Mandarin salamander

TOGO
Bubbling kassina
Goliath frog
Painted reed frog

TRINIDAD AND TOBAGO
Surinam toad

TUNISIA
Painted frog

TURKEY
Brown frog
European fire salamander
Fire-bellied toad
Great crested newt
Smooth newt

UGANDA
Bubbling kassina
Common plantanna (African
  clawed frog)
Painted reed frog

UKRAINE
European fire salamander
Great crested newt
Smooth newt

UNITED KINGDOM
Common plantanna (African
  clawed frog)
European fire salamander
Fire-bellied toad
Great crested newt
Smooth newt

Yellow-bellied toad

UNITED STATES
Arboreal salamander
Bullfrog
Cascade torrent salamander
Coastal giant salamander
Coastal tailed frog
Common plantanna (African
  clawed frog)
Dusky salamander
Eastern narrow-mouthed toad
Hellbender
Lesser siren
Marine toad
Mesoamerican burrowing toad
Mudpuppy
Plains spadefoot toad
Rocky Mountain tailed frog
Texas blind salamander
Three-toed amphiuma
Tiger salamander
Two-lined salamander

URUGUAY
Marine toad
Paradox frog

VENEZUELA
Marine toad
Paradox frog
Pyburn's pancake frog
Ruthven's frog
Surinam toad

VIETNAM
Ailao moustache toad
Annam broad-headed toad
Bana leaf litter frog
Mandarin salamander
Pointed-tongue floating frog

ZAMBIA
Bubbling kassina

Common plantanna (African
clawed frog)
Painted reed frog

Bubbling kassina
Common plantanna (African
clawed frog)

Common squeaker
Marbled snout-burrower
Painted reed frog

Index

Italic type indicates volume number; **boldface** type indicates entries and their pages; (ill.) indicates illustrations.

California red-legged frogs, 2: 292

Calls of frogs and toads. *See* Vocalization, in frogs and toads

Cape clawed toads. *See* Gill's plantannas

Cape ghost frogs, 1: 110, 112

Cape plantannas. *See* Gill's plantannas

Cascade torrent salamanders, 3: 473–75, 473 (ill.), 474 (ill.)

Cat-eyed frogs, 1: 77

Catholic frogs. *See* Crucifix frogs

Caucasian mud-divers. *See* Caucasus parsley frogs

Caucasian parsley frogs. *See* Caucasus parsley frogs

Caucasian salamanders, 3: 443

Caucasus parsley frogs, 1: 102, 103

Caudata. *See* Newts; Salamanders

Cave squeakers, 2: 314

Cayenne caecilians, 3: 533–35, 533 (ill.), 534 (ill.)

Centrolene ballux, 2: 248

Centrolene buckleyi, 2: 244

Centrolene geckoideum. See Pacific giant glass frogs

Centrolene gemmatum, 2: 248

Centrolene heloderma, 2: 248–49

Centrolene puyoense, 2: 248–49

Centrolenidae. *See* Glass frogs

Ceratophrys cornuta. See Surinam horned frogs

Ceylon caecilians, 3: 514–15, 514 (ill.), 515 (ill.)

Chachi treefrogs, 2: 260

Chalazodes bubble-nest frogs, 3: 356

Chile Darwin's frog, 2: 182–86

Chinese giant salamanders, 3: 419–20

Chinese salamanders, 3: 410

Chioglossa lusitanica. See Golden-striped salamanders

Chiricahua leopard frogs, 2: 292

Chirinda toads, 2: 199

Chubby frogs. *See* Malaysian painted frogs

Chytrid fungus, 1: 4, 11, 2: 203, 210, 216, 224 –225, 249, 264, 292

Cinnamon treefrogs. *See* Painted Indonesian treefrogs

Clawed frogs, 1: 62–76

Cloaca, 3: 411

    See also specific species

Clouded salamanders, 3: 410, 411

Coastal giant salamanders, 3: 427, 430–32, 430 (ill.), 431 (ill.)

Coastal tailed frogs, 1: 18

Cochranella anomala, 2: 248

Cochranella ignota. See Lynch's Cochran frogs

Cochranella luminosa, 2: 249

Cochranella saxiscandens, 2: 247

Colorado river toads, 2: 200

Colostethus caeruleodactylus. See Blue-toed rocket frogs

Common parsley frogs. *See* Parsley frogs

Common plantannas, 1: 64, 65, 67–69, 67 (ill.), 68 (ill.)

Common reed frogs. *See* Painted reed frogs

Common spadefoot frogs, 1: 127

Common squeakers, 2: 310–11, 313, 316–18, 316 (ill.), 317 (ill.)

Common treefrogs, 3: 353, 355

Congo eels. *See* Amphiumas

Congo snakes. *See* Amphiumas

Conondale gastric brooding frogs. *See* Northern gastric brooding frogs

Conraua goliath. See Goliath frogs

Cope's giant salamanders, 3: 427

Cope's gray treefrogs, 2: 261, 262, 3: 351

Cophixalus riparius. See Wilhelm rainforest frogs

Corisican midwife toads, 1: 48

Corroboree frogs, 1: 139, 143

Corsican painted frogs, 1: 45

Couch's spadefoot toads, 1: 97

Cricket frogs, 2: 310–22

Crowned forest frogs, 2: 310–11, 311

Crowned poison frogs. *See* Red-headed poison frogs

Crucifix frogs, 1: 124

Cryptobranchidae. *See* Asiatic giant salamanders; Hellbenders

Cryptobranchus alleganiensis. See Hellbenders

Cuban Iberian rain frogs, 1: 1

Cururo lesser escuerzos, 2: 156

Cururu toads. *See* Rococo toads

Cyclorana platycephala. See Water-holding frogs

Cynops pyrrhogaster. See Japanese fire-bellied newts

D

Danger, to frogs, 1: 4

Darwin's frogs, 2: 182–85, 186–89, 186 (ill.), 187 (ill.)

De Witte's snout-burrowers, 2: 326

Defense mechanisms, 1: 9–10

    See also specific species

Dendrobatidae. *See* Poison frogs

Dermophis mexicanus. See Mexican caecilians

Desert-living frogs, 3: 371

Desmognathus fuscus. See Dusky salamanders

Devil dogs. *See* Hellbenders

Dicamptodon tenebrosus. See Coastal giant salamanders

Dicamptodontidae. *See* Pacific giant salamanders

Hyla leucophyllata. See Hourglass treefrogs

Hylidae. *See* Amero-Australian treefrogs

Hymenochirus species. *See* Dwarf clawed frogs

Hynobiidae. *See* Asiatic salamanders

Hynobius retardatus. See Hokkaido salamanders

Hyperoliidae. *See* African treefrogs

Hyperolius viridiflavus. See Painted reed frogs

I

Iberian green frogs, *1:* 49

Iberian midwife toads, *1:* 44, 46–47

Iberian painted frogs, *1:* 47

Iberian parsley frogs, *1:* 102–3, 104

Iberian water frogs. *See* Iberian green frogs

Ichthyophiidae. *See* Asian tailed caecilians

Ichthyophis glutinosus. See Ceylon caecilians

Idaho giant salamanders, *3:* 427, 428

Imitating poison frogs, *2:* 219

Indian tiger frogs, *2:* 287

Introduced species, *1:* 4, 48–49, *2:* 157

IUCN Red List. *See* World Conservation Union (IUCN) Red List of Threatened Species

J

Jade treefrogs, *3:* 352

Jambato toads, *2:* 203

Japanese clawed salamanders, *3:* 411, 415–16, 415 (ill.), 416 (ill.)

Japanese fire-bellied newts, *3:* 455–56, 455 (ill.), 456 (ill.)

Japanese giant salamanders, *3:* 419–20, 422

Japanese treefrogs. *See* Kinugasa flying frogs

Java frogs. *See* Pointed-tongue floating frogs

Jurassic frogs. *See* Fossil frogs

K

Kaloula pulchra. See Malaysian painted frogs

Kassina senegalensis. See Bubbling kassinas

Kassinas, *3:* 335

　　See also Bubbling kassinas; Yellow-legged kassinas

Kerala caecilians, *3:* 517–21

Kinugasa flying frogs, *3:* 358–60, 358 (ill.), 359 (ill.)

Kirk's caecilians, *3:* 525–26, 525 (ill.), 526 (ill.)

Knysna banana frogs, *3:* 337

Korean salamanders, *3:* 410

L

La Palma glass frogs, *2:* 243, 246–47, 252–54, 252 (ill.), 253 (ill.)

Lake Oku clawed frogs, *1:* 66

Lake Zwai snout-burrowers. *See* Ethiopian snout-burrowers

Lamper eels. *See* Amphiumas

Lampreys. *See* Amphiumas

Lanza's alpine salamanders, *3:* 443

Large-spined bell toads, *1:* 29

Las Vegas leopard frogs, *2:* 291–92

Lazy toads, *1:* 77

Leaf-folding frogs, *3:* 335

Leaf litter frogs, *1:* 77, 79

Leiopelma hamiltoni. See Hamilton's frogs

Leiopelma pakeka. See Maud Island frogs

Leiopelmatidae. *See* New Zealand frogs

Leopard frogs, *2:* 287, 289–90

Lepidobatrachus laevis. See Budgett's frogs

Leptobrachium banae. See Bana leaf litter frogs

Leptodactylid frogs, *2:* 153–81

Leptodactylidae. *See* Leptodactylid frogs

Leptodactylus pentadactylus. See South American bullfrogs

Lesser sirens, *3:* 406–8, 406 (ill.), 407 (ill.)

Liangbei toothed toads, *1:* 80

Lichuan bell toads, *1:* 29

Limnodynastidae. *See* Australian ground frogs

Lithodytes lineatus. See Gold-striped frogs

Litoria caerulea. See Green treefrogs

Long-fingered slender toads, *2:* 205–7, 205 (ill.), 206 (ill.)

Long-fingered stream toads. *See* Long-fingered slender toads

Long-toed treefrogs, *3:* 337–38

Longdong stream salamanders, *3:* 410

Longnose stub-foot toads, *2:* 203

Loveridge's frogs, *1:* 128

Lungless salamanders, *3:* 476–93

Luzon bubble-nest frogs, *3:* 351, 354

Lynch's Cochran frogs, *2:* 242, 250–51, 250 (ill.), 251 (ill.)

M

Madagascar rain frogs, *3:* 392, 393–94

Madagascar reed frogs, *3:* 332

Madagascaran toadlets, *3:* 390–97

Malagasy variable reed frogs, *3:* 332

X

Xenopus laevis. See Common plantannas

Y

Yellow-bellied toads, *1:* 37–40, 37 (ill.), 38 (ill.)

Yellow-legged kassinas, *3:* 332

Yellow-legged treefrogs. *See* Yellow-legged kassinas

Yellow-striped reed frogs, *3:* 332

Yucatecan shovel-headed treefrogs, *2:* 276–77, 276 (ill.), 277 (ill.)

Yungas redbelly toads, *2:* 199, 200, 201

Yunnan moustache toads. *See* Ailao moustache toads

Z

Zimmermann's poison frogs, *2:* 219